A
MANUAL
FOR
DIRECT
ACTION

by

MARTIN OPPENHEIMER

and

GEORGE LAKEY

FOREWORD BY BAYARD RUSTIN

Drawings by Elsa Bailey

Chicago | QUADRANGLE BOOKS

A
MANUAL
FOR
DIRECT
ACTION

FOURTH PRINTING

to JAMES CHANEY
ANDREW GOODMAN
MICHAEL SCHWERNER

Foreword

Nonviolent direct action is not a new phenomenon in the world, nor is it any longer new in this country. Yet many of its current practitioners have come into various movements only recently. While their motives may be the highest, there are pitfalls in the path of those who would change society, above all pitfalls that can be avoided if one has some knowledge of them. The practitioners of nonviolence have had little time, until now, to write down or otherwise transmit their hard-won knowledge. All the more praiseworthy, then, is this book, which represents time deliberately taken off from the very activities which are described.

At long last here is a much-needed practical training manual for nonviolent direct action. I am deeply grateful that these two young sociologist-activists have taken the time to produce this book, particularly in this year when nonviolence is more and more under attack. The *Manual* may not be perfect, but it will probably be the pioneering endeavor in this field for some years to come. It should be carefully studied by every activist in civil rights and related causes. By this I don't mean to say that we have here a short-cut, a kind of "do-it-yourself," that can be committed to memory to solve all problems for all time. No one would wish this less than the authors. Rather, it is an outline, a guide to help those concerned with the problems of social change think through what they are confronting, both in terms of tactics and in terms of what change really means. While the emphasis is on civil rights in this country, a great deal of the information contained here has been gathered from other movements, for example from the Gandhian movement in India. In turn, the book can just as well be used by other movements. The labor movement, peace groups, community and neighborhood organizations, students, will all find something of value here. How valuably to apply it in any specific situation will depend on the insight and imagination which the practitioner brings with him.

This book should also be read by everyone interested in the
real meaning of the current civil rights struggle. Here one can
see unfolding within the context of training for action, the relationship of democracy and nonviolence to a truly human perspective for American society. When knowledge is limited to the
possession of a few, power, too, is centered, and decision-making
remains in the hands of an elite. But when knowledge is dissemi-
nated, as the authors intend it to be through the medium of this
book, power becomes more widely circulated, and the decision-
making monopoly is destroyed. Thus real education, as distinct
from learning formulas by rote, is a fundamentally democratizing
process.

In a similar way, nonviolence is inherently a democratizing
influence. For learning the techniques and philosophy of nonviolence means that the student must become intimately involved
with his subject, hence must become deeply aware of himself,
of the people who work with him and against him, and of his
environment. Such an awareness on the part of large numbers
of civil rights and other activists precludes or at least sharply
limits the development of narrow elites. The tactics and strategy
of nonviolence imply real education on the part of the user, and
education implies a development of thinking which leads to
involvement in decision-making by large numbers, hence to
democracy.

Within the last two or three years, civil rights activists have
moved increasingly into touch with deeper problems of the
community: poverty, housing, education, voter registration, police
relations, city planning, and social welfare policy have all come
in for attention, and I believe this will be increasingly true. In
that sense, "civil rights" has now gone beyond "race relations"
to confront many more fundamental issues. Summing up these
issues, I think it fair to say that civil rights has developed from
public accommodations to include public policy, or politics. On
some levels, for example the passage of the Civil Rights Act of
1964, in part due to the work of an active "Coalition of Conscience" in Washington, this political concern has already become

evident. But on the community level it has not often come to the surface. The authors, who have maintained day-to-day contact with the pulse of civil rights activity, have correctly gauged these new developments and have devoted an important chapter to the issue of community organization—what it means, how it is accomplished, and what its long-range implications for our society may be.

Not everyone will agree that nonviolent direct action is the most fruitful course of development for a better society in America. Many now feel that traditional nonviolent tactics have been outmoded, or made unnecessary, by the passage of progressive legislation. Others feel that the achievement of real gains requires such sweeping changes that nonviolence will not suffice. They call at minimum for armed defense, or even guerrilla warfare. It is true that the progress made in recent years is woefully inadequate. Yet if there is anything we have learned, it is that fundamental change for human betterment cannot take place if the changers dehumanize their opponents (hence also themselves) by doing them violence. In the face of the great way we still have to go, it seems premature to write nonviolence off as outmoded either because it has become unnecessary or because it has been proven inadequate. Of course, a concept of nonviolence that limits it to picket lines and sit-ins is far too narrow. For nonviolent direct action is not a closed book. It is a dynamic tool and a way of looking at life which can (and, I feel, ultimately must) affect many aspects of the human condition hardly touched upon by its practitioners at this early juncture. I believe the authors share this point of view and feel, accordingly, that this book is an experiment and an experience in that direction.

Events have ordained that the focus of this book be on civil rights in the United States. Yet it must be kept in mind that historically in this country nonviolence in civil rights has been profoundly influenced by pacifism and by the peace movement. Both of the authors, for example, had their first contact with the tactics and philosophy of nonviolence through the peace movement. So, indeed, have many of us. It continues to be our belief that the issue of human rights takes many forms: race relations is one such form, and international relations is another, but beneath the formal differences these issues are really inseparable. If they are separated today, it is an accident of history. In some fashion by no means clear to us at this point, I am confident that they will be joined ever more overtly in the years to come.

BAYARD RUSTIN

Introduction

This book is a product of the civil rights direct action movement. It has been put together so you can have, in one place, alternative courses of action and information on which you can base some of your thinking. It is not the Bible, however, and better things will come. As James Farmer has pointed out, we are in our infancy in nonviolent action. In the course of the revolution we may grow to maturity.

There are people who do not believe in manuals, or in training, or in thinking ahead, or in having a "program." They prefer to make all the mistakes for themselves. This book is for those who care more about the success of the struggle than about doing things on the spur of the moment. What we have put down here has been gleaned from the experience of civil rights and other movements; it includes some of the ideas of those who have learned painful lessons and want others to profit from them.

An important value of this manual is that it promotes democracy. The leader who alone understands the dynamics of a struggle and the techniques for waging it has a monopoly of power. Power flows to those who understand what is happening. When understanding and knowledge are shared, more persons can take a responsible part in decision-making. The movement need not flounder while the leader is in jail. Those readers who believe in democracy will see that a manual, and training, help to make a movement more democratic—and its participants more responsible.

Another reason for this book is that many of those who are now engaged in the struggle are young. Times are very different from the early forties when a few seasoned veterans of the peace and civil rights movements experimented with direct action tactics. Today much leadership comes from young people, angry with a society which preaches brotherhood and practices discrimination. Participants today frequently describe the struggle in *moral* terms: there is less theory than in the thirties. Since morality strikes deep, people can be deeply moved and very angry. Anger, like so many emotions, can be used constructively or destructively. The way indignation is channeled will depend partly on the readers of this manual.

The early campaigns for civil rights were led mostly by middle-class Negroes and whites. Now, more and more participants come from the working class and the unemployed. We know from study and experience that working class people, regardless of race, are readier to use violence than most middle class people. Because of the way children are brought up, because of the values they are taught, because of frustration piled on frustration, it is easier for some people to use violence in the struggle. This is another problem you must face. By sharing the knowledge gathered in this manual new recruits to the movement will come to a better understanding of what is happening, and to a more positive reaction to the events of the day.

We have all seen people, angered by a piece of machinery which would not work, give it a kick or try to force it by brute strength. And we have seen others inspect the machine closely, find the right lever, and set it running again.

This manual begins with an examination of that complicated piece of social machinery, the community, and points to some of the levers which can be used to bring about change. But the levers will not be moved without organization. Education of the participants is essential if the movement is to be democratic and aware of its direction.

Preparing for direct action means choosing effective tactics and training. The manual will also share what is known about non-violent defense. Arrest, court procedures, and prison, too, require preparation. The issue of how far nonviolence should be taken, and whether armed self-defense makes sense, will also be discussed.

Finally there are appendices with interesting reference material recommended for jail and other leisure reading.

Since much of this manual is focused on direct action, which sometimes involves civil disobedience—hence violation of the law, the authors have been charged with "advocating" breaking the law. We want to make it clear at the outset that we neither advocate nor advise breaking the law. What we have attempted to do is to suggest a variety of tactics and strategies that can be used in the course of struggling for a better way of life. We believe that, whenever possible, direct action should take place within the law. In this country most direct action is in fact protected by law, and arrest and violence frequently occur because the law is not being followed by law enforcement officers themselves.

There are places and times when law so abuses the inherent rights of people that the only way to make grievances known, and begin to create a more just situation, is to violate the law. Every individual must decide for himself just when such a point is reached in society. We do not presume to make that decision for others, nor do we presume to choose tactics of direct action for others. The final choice is yours.

Contents

A
MANUAL
FOR
DIRECT
ACTION

1 / THE CIVIL RIGHTS MOVEMENT IN AMERICAN HISTORY

Most of those now active in civil rights and other direct action movements in this country were born in the mid-1940's. They know about World War II, the depression, and the social protest of the New Deal era only through the pages of history textbooks. About the great tradition of Negro protest which led to the present movement, they know even less, for it is hardly mentioned in most high school and even college history courses.

There is no real "beginning" to the history of Negro protest; it is, of course, rooted in Africa. Slave revolts were common occurrences aboard ship, throughout the West Indies (resulting in the independence of the island of San Domingo), in the plantation South, and even in the North prior to the Civil War. Many of these revolts were integrated, involving white indentured servants and poor farmers—the famous raid on Harpers Ferry by John Brown was also interracial. The happy slave dwelling amidst the scent of magnolia blossoms and mint juleps is a myth.

After the Civil War, freed Negroes had some measure of political rights in the South, which was occupied by federal troops until 1877. They elected a number of Negro congressmen and two senators (both from Mississippi). In general, Negroes holding public office during the Reconstruction era performed well, again contrary to myth, especially when compared with the behavior of other public figures in a time of widespread corruption and public immorality. After the Compromise of 1876, which made Hayes President of the United States, federal troops were withdrawn from the South and Negroes began to lose many of their hard-won rights. But it was not until the break-up of the frequently integrated Populist, or People's, party, in 1896 that Jim Crow laws as we know them today began to be passed. In some states such laws were not passed until about 1910. With the passing of the Populist movement, sometimes called the "Agrarian Crusade," came the end of Negro politics and of the two-party system in the South until our own time.

The disillusionment of many Negroes with current politics at that time, resulting partly from the collapse of Populism and partly from the desertion of the Negro by Northern liberalism, led to the rise of Booker T. Washington as a popular Negro leader. Washington became a symbol of non-involvement in integrationist agitation, and his followers, informally organized into what became known as the "Tuskegee Machine" (after the college which Washington helped to found), emphasized vocational training, hard work, and keeping one's nose clean.

NEGROES MOVE TO THE BIG CITY

As Negroes moved into Northern cities around the turn of the century (in part because of the collapse of the cotton market), they came into contact with many new ideas. The philosophy of Booker T. Washington was no longer adequate for many, and the result was the formation, in 1905, of the "Niagara Movement" by W. E. B. DuBois. This was the forerunner of the National Association for the Advancement of Colored People, which was organized in its present form in 1910. The NAACP quickly became active in drives to establish laws against lynching, and pushed an integrationist viewpoint.

World War I took many Negroes to France, where they came into contact with an entirely different way of handling the "race problem"—the French treated Negroes as equals. They also met Negroes from Africa who conveyed to them many of the African ideas of independence beginning to take shape at that time. The result was that many returning "doughboys" were unwilling to accept their pre-war status as second-class citizens. A series of racial incidents in a number of cities took place in the summer of 1919, frequently involving Negro ex-soldiers, and race riots broke out. This became known as "Red Summer."

Some disillusionment with the "gradual" tactics of the NAACP resulted. This, together with a new sense of race pride brought back by the ex-soldiers, contributed to the rise of the Universal Negro Improvement Association, led by Marcus Garvey, a Jamaican. Garveyism, as it became known, was a nationalistic, "back-to-Africa" movement which recruited hundreds of thousands of Negroes to its ranks in the few years it was able to command attention. But Garvey had not trained his followers; the movement was authoritarian, and once Garvey was deported (as a result of a mail fraud conviction) his lieutenants began to squabble and the movement died. The present Nation of Islam, however, can be traced historically and ideologically to Garveyism.

All of these events in the development of the civil rights movement took place while the American Negro was moving in large numbers from the country to the city, and from the South to the North. With this movement to find jobs and a better way of life (a movement which continues today), came all of the social problems which we have come to associate with "urbanization": family break-ups, crime, delinquency, bad housing, unemployment, poor schools (not that country schools had been any better), and the evils of the urban political machine. But at least two factors served to balance this picture to some degree for the Negro: contact with new ideas, new visions of equality; and contact with and membership in trade unions. Both factors broadened the cultural and political horizon of the ex-farmer population, and some unions (as well as some churches) trained many of today's leaders of Negro protest.

The depression, which began in 1929, hit the Negro particularly hard. Several important developments paralleled the New Deal decade (1932 to 1941). First, the attempts made by the Roosevelt administration to solve the depression problem, even though inadequate, swung the Negro voter into the Democratic party column in large numbers in the North (he did not vote in large numbers in the South anyway). Second, some Negroes engaged in a brief flirtation with the Communist party, but this did not last long; the zigs and zags of party policy in these years disillusioned most Negroes. They gradually understood that "The Negro Question" was secondary to the current needs of Soviet foreign policy. Third, the process of urbanization continued. With it came the confidence of numbers gathered in one place; the growth of a better educated and financially more independent middle and professional class to serve the large numbers; and the growth of a powerful bloc of voters who were able to obtain favors.

Success in obtaining small favors leads to demands for bigger favors. These favors lead to a better way of life, at least for some; to an education which gives a broader view, and thus to still wider demands. Morale improves, committees and lobbies are formed, and still more demands are made and achieved. All of these pressures had an effect upon the federal executive, judiciary, and legislature, and in turn these branches of government, by taking measures to improve the lot of the Negro, have provoked pressures for still further equality in citizenship.

In 1941, just prior to our entry into World War II, A. Philip Randolph, head of the Brotherhood of Sleeping Car Porters, organized the March on Washington Movement. The threat of the march—which never came off—led to the signing, by President Roosevelt, of an executive order establishing a federal Fair Employment Practices Commission. In 1949 President Harry

S. Truman signed another executive order putting equality of treatment in the armed forces into effect "as rapidly as possible." Within about four years this was accomplished. Other orders, for example, an Interstate Commerce Commission ruling forbidding discrimination in interstate bus travel, followed.

In the courts, the NAACP bore the brunt of the action in a long series of educational cases which finally resulted in the famous Supreme Court decision in *Brown* v. *Board of Education* on May 17, 1954, stating that "separate educational facilities are inherently unequal." A year later the Court supplemented that decision with an order requiring school authorities to begin steps to comply "with all deliberate speed." Unfortunately, the emphasis so far has been on the deliberate, not on the speed.

In the Congress, the first civil rights bill since 1875 was passed on September 9, 1957, under President Eisenhower, and in the summer of 1960 a second bill was passed under the Eisenhower administration. The third bill, passed in 1964, is discussed in an appendix to this *Manual*.

NEGROES RESPOND TO WORLD WAR II

World War II, like World War I, had important repercussions in the Negro community. First, it alleviated the depression to a large degree, giving Negroes a chance at a limited number of skilled jobs. Second, it again thrust Negro soldiers, even though they were still segregated, into contact with new situations and new ideas. Third, it once more showed American Negroes the hypocrisy of a nation which claimed to be fighting against fascism and for democracy, yet failed to treat a tenth of its population as first-class citizens.

Randolph's March on Washington Movement (which, by the way, was the first American Negro protest action officially to endorse the principle of nonviolent direct action) led to a series of efforts, even during the war, to protest discrimination. On June 16, 1942, for example, during a Madison Square Garden rally in New York, lights in Harlem were turned out in response to Randolph's call. During that summer, the still intact MOWM organization organized several marches to protest the execution of a Negro, Odell Walker, in Virginia. That same year, the Congress of Racial Equality (CORE) was founded in Chicago. Organized mainly by white pacifists, it took over many of the principles laid down by Randolph for MOWM. It went immediately to work in the field of public accommodations and began to stage the first sit-ins at restaurants. CORE's experience in these early years was to come in handy later. In 1947, the Fellowship of Reconciliation, out of which CORE had developed, cooperated with CORE in recruiting twenty-three persons who carried out a project called a "Freedom Ride" in the upper South to test an early Supreme Court decision on interstate travel. In 1948, partly to offset the possible effect of Henry Wallace's Progressive party campaign, both major parties put anti-discrimination planks into their platforms.

As the Cold War iced over the American scene in the late 1940's, open protest slowed down. The prosperity of most Americans also helped to gloss over the continuing problem of "The Other America," including Negroes. Still, even the Cold War served to focus some attention on discrimination, for, as the U.S. and the U.S.S.R. competed for the favors of African, Asian, and Latin American nations (many predominantly nonwhite), our treatment of both Americans and visiting persons of color became a daily scandal on the front pages of the world press. As their African cousins began to overcome centuries of foreign oppression, more and more American Negroes asked themselves when their own yoke would be removed.

On December 1, 1955, Mrs. Rosa Parks, a Negro seamstress and formerly the secretary of the local NAACP, boarded a bus in downtown Montgomery, Alabama. She was tired and sat down in the first seat behind the section reserved for whites. Several white passengers boarded. The bus driver ordered her and three other Negro passengers to move back. She refused and was arrested. In protest, the vast majority of the Negro community refused to ride Montgomery buses from December 5 until November 14, 1956, and walked to work or organized car pools. They returned to the buses only after a Supreme Court decision on November 13, 1956, declared Alabama's state and local bus segregation laws unconstitutional.

This was the Montgomery Bus Boycott, the first major campaign in the nonviolent direct action movement which is still underway. The campaign catapulted onto the stage of American history a young Baptist minister, the Rev. Martin Luther King, Jr., who soon became the symbol of American Negro protest throughout the world. After Montgomery it seemed only a matter of time before a major revival of Negro protest would take place. Lobbying and court battles seemed outmoded or overly slow in achieving significant progress, and King's tactics seemed both an alternative and a way for the ordinary citizen to become involved in the struggle.

Late in the fall of 1956 a group of Northern Negroes, encouraged by whites close to a variety of pacifist organizations, and organized by A. Philip Randolph, called for a massive "Prayer Pilgrimage" to the Lincoln Memorial in Washington. This became the first of a series of revivals of the March on Washington idea, which reached its high point in the massive march of August, 1963. The 1956 effort was not particularly successful—with a Negro population in Washington of some 400,000 at that time, only 20,000 attended the ceremonies. One observer pointed out that it would take more than prayer to move the nation's white power structure.

YOUTH JOINS THE MOVEMENT

On October 25, 1958, and again on April 18, 1959, the idea of the march was repeated, but with emphasis on youth. These were the two Youth Marches for Integrated Schools, organized chiefly by Bayard Rustin, a Negro radical pacifist with many years of experience in mass movements. The two youth marches turned out, respectively, 8,000 and 25,000 young people, and contributed significantly to the continuing growth of civil rights concern on American college campuses. But a specific technique which people could use in their own communities to get things done had not yet been widely developed.

In 1957, in Oklahoma City, a fourteen-year-old Negro girl, Barbara Ann Posey, joined the NAACP's Youth Council. There she learned the story of Rev. King and the Montgomery Bus Boycott. She went to New York City to attend a youth rally and was much impressed with that city's integrated facilities. When she returned to Oklahoma City she was determined to do something about locally segregated facilities. A sit-in on August 19, 1958, was the result. This appears to have been the first formal sit-in by predominantly Negro students, and it resulted in the desegregation of all but one of the five stores selected for action. On Sunday, August 24, 1958, twenty pairs of Negro youths visited twenty white churches; they were refused at only three, making Oklahoma City the first community to have a "kneel-in," or "pray-in," though neither of these terms had been invented yet.

News of the Oklahoma City sit-ins spread to other NAACP Youth Councils. Sit-ins took place in Wichita and Kansas City, Kansas; and in Enid, Tulsa, and Stillwater, Oklahoma, that year. In Tallahassee there was a bus boycott, though with less result than in Montgomery. Other local demonstrations protested resistance to school integration, especially in Virginia. But the sit-in idea did not catch hold for another year and a half.

At 4:30 P.M. on Feb. 1, 1960, four Negro students at North Carolina A & T College in Greensboro entered the F. W. Woolworth store in downtown Greensboro and deliberately sat down at the lunch counter. They waited for service knowing that Negroes traditionally were not served. They were not served. They sat and waited until the store closed for the day, and left. The following day they were back with other students. Girls from Bennett College soon joined in. As crowds of whites began to threaten the Negro students in the store, the four boys realized they had bitten off quite a chunk. They went to the head of the local NAACP chapter for help. He called the CORE national office in New York. CORE immediately sent a field secretary who organized workshops in nonviolence.

The Greensboro action was quickly picked up by newspapers and radio, and within a few days Durham and Winston-Salem students were staging their own "sit-ins." Within two weeks sit-ins were taking place in Virginia and South Carolina, and within two months the movement (for such it was) spread to nearly eighty cities as far removed as Xenia, Ohio, and Sarasota, Florida. Some facilities in six Southern communities were desegregated quickly, and more were to follow. But more than 1,000 students and their sympathizers were arrested, and hundreds were harassed in one way or another, including tear gas, police dogs, burning cigars on clothing, beatings, and suspension or expulsion from college.

The sit-in movement continued to spread and gained varying degrees of success in more than 130 communities in the upper and middle South. Sit-ins were succeeded by other direct action techniques—movie stand-ins, church pray-ins, beach wade-ins. But no integration was achieved in any of the deep Southern states of South Carolina, Georgia, Alabama, Mississippi, or Louisiana at that time. The "easy" victories had been achieved; now the students were up against the hard core of segregation, and the sit-ins and other actions to secure integrated public accommodations began to bog down.

The 1960 Sit-In Movement was, according to most observers of civil rights history in this country, a turning point. It marked the beginning of a new wave of Negro protest, one which is still underway today. It also put nonviolent direct action on "the agenda" of social change in a wider sense for Americans. Perhaps less important in the long run, but certainly critical for the history of this decade, the sit-ins indirectly contributed what was probably the decisive margin in the narrow victory won by the late President Kennedy in November, 1960. Many observers believe that the personal intervention of Kennedy on behalf of Rev. Martin Luther King, Jr., after King was arrested in the course of demonstrations in Atlanta that October, was crucial in swinging Negro votes to the Kennedy-Johnson ticket. Several states in which the Negro vote was probably decisive went for the winning ticket by very small margins—notably Texas, South Carolina, and Illinois.

SNCC IS ORGANIZED

In April, 1960 the Student Nonviolent Coordinating Committee (SNCC) was organized in Raleigh, North Carolina. For more than a year, SNCC was chiefly a coordinating group. Then, as it began to grapple with the problems of segregation in the deep South, it began to develop its own staff and full-time volunteer organization, apart from its participating member groups. This was a necessary step forward as the integrationist struggle moved from the campus and from a primary interest in public accommodations into the Negro community, and into contact with the basic problems of that community.

It was the Freedom Rides of 1961, the bus rides to test inter-state transportation integration, which acted as the bridge to this new emphasis. For the Freedom Rides—the first organized by CORE, and others later in the summer organized by SNCC—took students from the campus and put them in touch with the wider Negro community. This contact quickly developed into a concern with one of the chief problems of the Negro community in the South—voting and registration to vote. SNCC decided that voter registration efforts would be next on the agenda of the civil rights movement in the South.* This effort, which began as early as the fall of 1960 in the thinking of some SNCC people, picked up steam after the 1961 Freedom Rides and received most of its public acclaim during the summer of 1964. Hundreds of students from all over the United States went to Mississippi to help in voter registration and the associated "freedom school" projects organized by the Council of Federated Organizations (COFO), a group composed of CORE, SNCC, the NAACP, and Rev. King's Southern Christian Leadership Conference (SCLC). As we know, three of the workers in this project, to whom this book is dedicated, were killed in the campaign to bring civil rights and liberties to the people of Mississippi. The repercussions of that summer are still being felt as this book goes to press. The bombing of churches and other centers of Freedom Schools and voter registration activity, the intimidation of civil rights workers and potential and actual registered voters, and shootings into the homes of leading figures in the Freedom Movement continue.

In the North, too, a shift in tactics has occurred. In the early

* For more information on the history of SNCC see Howard Zinn's *SNCC: The New Abolitionists,* Boston, The Beacon Press, 1964.

days of the Southern sit-ins, most Northern civil rights actions took the form of picketing to support the Southern movement. Soon, however, these support groups began to act on problems in their own communities. But, partly reflecting the primarily middle class and student composition of direct action groups in these early days, these efforts were mainly directed toward public accommodations. In the North this meant integration of facilities that required the expenditure of money: clubs, swimming pools, and above all suburban middle-income and upper-income housing. But in the effort to integrate basically middle class facilities, it became necessary to recruit larger numbers of people, especially Negroes, to gain more power. And as larger numbers of Negroes were recruited into the active movement, organizations such as CORE became more working class in composition. The new composition was quickly reflected in new demands: improved housing, better schools in Negro neighborhoods, more jobs. Just as in the South SNCC was thrown into the Negro community in its effort to register voters, so in the urban North CORE began to establish more direct contact with the urban Negro ghettos in order to involve the larger numbers of people needed to move toward the newer goals. Community organization became part and parcel of American "race relations."

Civil rights today moves beyond mere integration *into* existing American society. By the nature of the fact that civil rights involves basic issues confronting *all* Americans (jobs, automation, education, housing, urban renewal, and, through all of these, politics), the movement now goes beyond the relations between the races and involves the relationship of men to all other men, and the relationship between all men and the basic decision-making processes of our society.

Unfortunately, the shift in focus by the nonviolent direct action civil rights organizations to the Negro community and its problems has been slow and relatively recent. Meanwhile, the civil rights movement has contributed to raising the sights of American Negroes, but without always succeeding in attaining the demands of the day. The resistance of local and even national power structures to change continues, and while civil rights groups may be able to achieve lunch counter integration, it is another thing to achieve decent schools, housing, and jobs. These demands involve many more changes in the basic rules of our society. Above all, the demand for jobs in a nation where the entire job market (even for whites) is unable to keep up with an expanding population, a market which within a few years may even be decreasing, involves fundamental issues that challenge the very foundations of our economy. Success cannot be easy, yet these are the very issues which are closest to the everyday needs of the Negro ghettos, both North and South.

This "revolution of rising expectations" has met with little real success despite the efforts of civil rights groups, and it has frequently resulted in disappointment, frustration, and despair. It is a despair rooted in our basic social institutions, but it has been channeled into the civil rights groups themselves, who seem to be immediately responsible for the lack of results. Above all, it has questioned the tactics—nonviolent direct action—of these groups. Today, alternative tactics are being widely advocated, and new groups are coming forward to claim the allegiance of the Negro community. These groups, generally called "nationalist" or "separatist," will no more be able to solve the basic problems of our society than those which have gone before. Yet, because they claim to be "militant," and because they are prepared to use violence, they give the impression of being able to intimidate and coerce local white power structures. Is armed defense, possibly even guerrilla warfare, the ultimate answer to the Negro's problems? Or can the nonviolent direct action organizations succeed in marshaling enough power to confront the basic problems of our society so that they can be solved in another way?

2 / THE COMMUNITY

You act and react, as a civil rights worker or as a member of other movements, within a series of communities. There is the greater community of the Western world. There are smaller communities such as the family, small groups, cliques. But for our purposes the community in which we are interested is that of the city or town, as it exists within a state and region. While no two communities are ever the same, some general rules do apply to most communities that exist within a modern industrial society.

Whether you are engaged in citizenship education or sit-ins, it is important to know the community in which you act. In terms of an ongoing, organized campaign, it is crucial to be aware of a series of conditions: Who has the power? What is the relationship of forces, both racial and otherwise? What is the economy like? If you are considering a boycott, it is important to know what role the Negro community plays in relation to the stores being boycotted. In a city like Atlanta, downtown stores do not depend much on Negro trade because Negroes tend to deal with well-established concerns within their own community. A boycott will be difficult. In a city like Nashville, where the Negro community is located not far from the center-city business district, and where whites have been moving to the suburbs rapidly, the business district is heavily dependent on Negro trade. A boycott may be crucial.

Another example which shows the importance of analyzing the power structure of the community is the role played in the community by the state government. That a city is also a state capital may change its reactions—state legislators may take a hand (usually negative) in the struggle. Or, because a state government has differences with a local power structure, it may play a role in the struggle where otherwise it might stay out. You may have to contend with (or have the tacit alliance of) state troopers.

You should also be aware that outside business interests
may be crucial in the decision-making process of the local power
structure. Actually, the real financial—hence decision-making—
power may not be inside the community at all; it may be located
in a distant city and state. If this is the case, allies in that distant city may need to be called on to lend support in a variety
of ways.

How will you find this out? * You should consult, first, a
statewide directory of companies, which can be obtained from
the chamber of commerce or the library. Then, when you have
located the companies important in your community, you should
look them up in *Moody's Industrial Manual,* also to be found
in the library. Here you can locate the home office of the
company. Then you can learn the names and addresses of the
officers of the company by consulting *Poor's Registry of Executives and Directors.* Local companies can also be checked in
such references as *Moody's Bank and Finance Manual, Moody's
Utilities Manual,* and *Moody's Transportation Manual.* This
is only a beginning, and much more can be done to uncover
the real nature of a local power structure. In focusing upon the
local side of the power structure, sources of information also
include back copies of local newspapers, local almanacs, chamber
of commerce figures, census data (available from the Bureau of
the Census, U.S. Department of Commerce, or at most large
libraries), and interviews with local business, labor, and political figures (preferably before they know why you are really
there). Do not neglect looking at the society pages to find out
which families "count" in decision-making processes, and do
not forget to inspect the forces moving within the Negro
community.

What factors should you be looking for when you make this
"social inventory?"

---

* For a more thoroughgoing outline of this problem, see Jack Minnis, *The
Care and Feeding of Power Structures* (mimeo), Students for a Democratic
Society, 1608 West Madison Street, Chicago, Ill.

WHO HAS THE POWER IN THE COMMUNITY?

That is, which people, families, and business concerns, which politicians, ministers, and educators have the authority to make decisions which influence the behavior of other individuals or groups of things? Generally speaking, the real decision-making power will tend to overlap with "society." Not all people in "society" have power, and not all power people are in "society," but as a group they will overlap. The elite (and this is just as true in the Negro community) will have gone to certain schools and universities, will live in a certain area considered more desirable, will belong to certain social clubs, will attend certain churches, and, above all, will be concentrated in certain occupations and professions: directors of large business (smaller in smaller communities), financiers, and the lawyers who serve them constitute the "power elite" of a community.

The elite will vary, of course, with the kind of community—in an area of large plantation-type agriculture, there will be one kind of elite. In a more commercial and industrial area, there will be another. Important parts of the decision-making elite may not live in the city. Above all, it is important to remember that elites do not always agree among themselves. They have interests which differ and sometimes conflict. These differences and conflicts can be "used" by the smart civil rights worker.

(Example: Generally it is wise to try to boycott all stores, even when some stores are prepared to give in to demands on equal hiring and serving. The managers who are willing to give in will then pressure the more stubborn ones.)

It is generally necessary to deal with the power structure when raising civil rights demands, and it is important that the power structure be aware of the issues. Frequently the biracial commission or mayor's committee will channel information from the civil rights groups through to the power structure, and this is valuable. A power structure which is ignorant of the issues and of the nature of the opposition cannot make realistic decisions in a conflict situation. Nor can the movement act realistically unless it is aware of what the power structure is likely to do. Conflict is ultimately the test through which both sides learn about each other, and this is one of the best aspects of the dispute. The century-old silence between the races (and ignorance about real feelings despite all the talk that "we know our nigras") is being broken, because conflict talks.

WHAT ARE THE RELATIONS BETWEEN THE RACIAL GROUPS?

In making out a social inventory it is crucial to know what the situation is, and has been, before moving on. What rights do Negroes have? How did they get these rights? Can Negroes be policemen? Firemen? If so, only in Negro sections? Who votes? Who rides buses? Who can go to the movies? Balcony only for Negroes? Which Negro businesses are really white controlled? Which churches? Which politicians? Which school board members?

The most important factor, again, in determining the present relationship of the races (and making a prediction of the degree of resistance to future change) is the proportion of Negroes in the population. The more Negroes, the more resistance, except in *large* cities.

You must be aware of what you're getting into. (You don't need training manuals for the easy situation!) As with any exercise, you practice the way you play, and winners tend to be people who practice hard and know the angles. The deep South particularly is no affair for amateurs.

WHO ARE YOUR FRIENDS AND WHO ARE YOUR OPPONENTS?

You can assume very little when you first go into an unfamiliar community. Some spade-work may have been done by someone before you, but this is frequently not the case. Education matters less than an ability to understand and communicate. The noisiest civil rights revolutionist may only be telling you what he thinks you want to hear, or what he thinks you ought to know. Some ministers, schoolteachers, and businessmen in the Negro community depend on segregation for their living. Others do not. People with independent incomes (or no incomes) will tend to be readier to act than those who depend on others and are insecure. Juvenile gangs, if approached in the right way, can be given a new purpose in life and can be valuable allies—but do not expect them to become nonviolent angels overnight. Furthermore, traditional educational methods (lectures) may not work and you will have to try new and ingenious methods of teaching and training.

It is important to try to involve segments of the white community. In Charlotte, North Carolina, the involvement of white Unitarians finally broke resistance to the sit-ins. Frequently a gesture will help: Is there a union organizing campaign going on? These are potential allies. You cannot expect allies to come to you simply because our cause is just. Everyone has prejudices of many kinds—the thing to do is to limit a person's chances to find reasons for bringing these prejudices out into the open. This is an important reason for nonviolence—it makes good public relations sense because it limits the chances for finding reasons to be against the movement. At the same time we cannot compromise, because not only will we lose thereby but the Negro community, whose involvement is crucial, will be antagonized. So to maximize allies, don't antagonize—but don't compromise.

When going to other organizations for help, it is important to know how policy is made: by a few leaders, or at membership meetings, or otherwise? And can these organizations really be of help in the long run, or will they "use" the cause to promote a particular brand of politics? Will a change in national policy force them to abandon you? Your community study should show which organizations, churches, and unions are likely to help (based on their past record). All groups in a community (regardless of type—even Alcoholics Anonymous), as well as all individuals, fall into one of the following classes:

1. Active associates and friends in the cause.
2. Support, but not active participation. Financial help.
3. Moral support, some individuals giving money.
4. Neutral—organization divided evenly.
5. Hostile, but not active . . . wait and see.
6. Actively hostile (Citizens Councils, Klan, etc.).

Your primary job is (a) to decide which of the above is your target group in a particular campaign; your secondary task is (b) to move everybody one step up. Each of the groups will require a somewhat different approach (to be discussed in the section on public relations).

Where allies are concerned, your chief problems are fear and apathy. We can't say much about fear. This is something you'll have to deal with depending upon the situation. Alternative ways of earning a living and finding a roof can't always be created (e.g., Tent City in Tennessee). But apathy may be due to bad planning, poor preparation, poor timing, and/or poor leadership. People declare a kind of mental sit-in when they are confronted with dictatorial "leaders" who keep the decision-making process clasped tightly to their own bosoms. People who don't trust the rank-and-file sufficiently to let them know what is happening or to let them have a say in it, don't deserve to be trusted, and apathy sooner or later results. Partly it results because dictators talk a big game but don't produce—their failure to produce is due to the fact that they make mistakes, and this happens because they don't listen to anybody, or listen only to friends who agree with them. Totalitarianism simply is not the most efficient way of "getting things done" in the long run. Sooner or later leaders become isolated, and the organization degenerates into a clique.

WHAT SHOULD YOU BASE YOUR STRATEGY ON?

Strategy must be guided by your own situation, and cannot be taken out of a book. There are, however, three particularly important considerations you should take into account. First, *the political awareness of the Negro community*. In some places the Negro community is so frightened, apathetic, or lacking in civic awareness that the first step may be a voter registration campaign. Communication and concern can thus be built about the major issues facing Negroes.

Second, *the number of Negroes in proportion to whites*. If there is a large number of Negroes in proportion to whites, the white community will feel especially threatened in a physical sense. The strategy will have to take this into account and prepare for a longer and tougher campaign. Boycotts obviously work better in a situation of numerical superiority.

Third, *the political situation*. It may be such that while the town is bitterly opposed to the movement, the governor of the state is a potential ally. Large demonstrations may be required to flag his attention, or to put him on the political spot. On the other hand, the town may make concessions which the state may not, because of political ambition by the governor so that he must cater to segregationists, or for some other reason. In such a case, it would be better not to get the state (and possible state police violence) involved.

The main point is that what works in one situation may not in another, and massive demonstrations may not always be tactically best.

SHOULD OUTSIDERS BE BROUGHT IN?

If there is one "rule" which has been consistently true over the years in different movements, it is this: the presence of "outsiders" helps to solidify resistance locally against the movement that uses these outsiders. Opponents use the presence of outsiders as a propaganda weapon against the campaigners. In the civil rights struggle, outsiders help segregationists maintain their myth that local Negroes are not really in the struggle of their own will, and consequently the status quo is not unjust after all. Some civil rights groups have therefore taken great pains to identify themselves as local. In one case in the upper South, leaders of a sit-in asked a publicity-conscious organizer to go back to his national office, and issued statements that they were not connected with his organization.

Organizers from outside may sometimes be necessary. When there is no local movement, or if the movement is in trouble and lacking important skills in direct action, there is often no choice but to bring in outside help. But this should be done realizing that there will be some ill effects. If a movement in a town is healthy and has good leadership, it can be a real disservice for leadership to call for "1,000 supporters" from a nearby city to come and "help" them. (There are things outsiders can do which minimize the bad effects, such as raising money or picketing their local affiliate of the demonstrators' target. Direct action can also be taken at the state or national capital.)

One more reason why it is not necessarily helpful to have outside leaders or numbers of demonstrators is that in the last analysis no one can *give* anyone else freedom. Following the Freedom Rides, valuable though they were in many ways, Negroes went back to segregated practices in some towns because they had not won the freedom for themselves.

There are times, and campaigns, such as the Council of Federated Organizations campaign in Mississippi in the summer of 1964, when a conscious decision is made to bring numbers of outsiders into the situation. In Mississippi the total impact on the nation was held to be more significant than the negative impact on local white inhabitants. In fact, the negative impact only helped to symbolize the lawlessness and nonparticipation in American democracy of the state of Mississippi.

HOW IS THE STRUGGLE LIKELY TO PROCEED?

Most direct action campaigns go through several stages. If we label them according to the reactions of the opponent, we have: (1) indifference; (2) active antagonism; (3) disunity;

and (4) negotiation. The first stage, indifference, has already passed in many areas because of the national impact of the struggle and wide press coverage. Even in towns where no direct action has taken place, there is no longer much indifference and lines have been drawn. The town may be edgy and the power structure may, at the onset of demonstrations, immediately respond with active antagonism. However, if you are working in a town where indifference is the first response, you can use the time gained to good advantage in tightening up organizational effectiveness.

The second stage, active antagonism, is the period when the tide often runs highest against the movement. It may be long or short, depending on a number of factors including how deeply committed the opponents are to segregation. There is a tendency at this time for communication between Negro and white to cease.

This stage is crucial, for it is here that a lot of learning takes place. In the heat of conflict people are hypersensitive to the actions of the other side. Actions which confirm the prejudices of the opponent will be seized upon and magnified; those which counter the prejudices will have more impact than ordinarily. Disorderly, undisciplined direct action will confirm the belief that "those Negroes aren't ready for freedom," while courageously facing troopers without wavering will refute, among at least some, the belief that "Negroes, like animals, will be scared away by a show of force."

Some of your forces will at this point question the usefulness of continuing the struggle—"we are worse off now than when we started." They are right in the sense that, if the campaign stopped now, Negro and white communities would be further apart than before you began. But if the struggle continues it will pass into stage three. Sometimes a "cooling-off period" takes place before stage three; some negotiating, usually not fruitful, often goes with the "cooling-off" period.

The third stage, disunity of the opponent, is the fruit of what came earlier. Demonstrations have been resumed. More and more of the people in or near the power structure will have doubts about the rightness of the measures they are using to beat you down. They will begin to reconsider their position. White moderates can play an important role here, setting up lines of communication between the civil rights forces and the opponents, and finding arguments (including economic) which make it seem unreasonable for the power structure to hold out much longer. The discussions among the opponents and the moderates often go on without the knowledge of the civil rights leaders; unless there is a dramatic breakthrough, like a prominent minister's preaching on your behalf, you may not be aware that this stage is actually occurring until it is finished.

The fourth stage, a second and more realistic round of negotiations, is also an important one, for poor negotiation can bring a return to open conflict. The negotiator should try to do two things: (1) describe the results of change as *less* threatening than the opponents suppose, and (2) describe the results of *not* changing the practices as *more* threatening than the results of change.

One way to show that change would not be threatening is to bring with you illustrations of successes in other places. Sometimes opponents will agree to have a trial run of the change; this must be done in good faith, however, without using it to sound out customers or citizens by telling them, "We're just trying this thing out—what's your reaction?" Experience shows that polling before desegregation brings many more negative reactions than actually occur when the change takes place.

The negotiator also needs to describe the results of *not* making concessions. He makes it clear that these results (more demonstrations, etc.) will occur if a solution cannot be worked out, but he also makes clear his great reluctance to use them unless forced to do so. Experience shows that the negotiator is not usually effective if he is hostile and uses the sanctions as a threat to the opponent—"You give what we want or you'll get what's coming to you!" The tone should be friendly and firm.

If the opponent is using excuses like "This isn't the time to do it," "We can't move too quickly in these matters," it is wise to get him *on record* officially in favor of fair play practices *in general.* He will then have difficulty later evading this commitment. The negotiators should try to foresee all possible evasions which the opponent might introduce, and anticipate them, using workshops and socio-drama to brief the negotiating team.

In this description of the four stages of direct action we have assumed that preliminary negotiations did take place and that the authorities (official, employer, manager) refused to give in. There are two important reasons for holding preliminary negotiations: first, they may solve the problem (some towns have agreed after witnessing nearby cities in the throes of direct action); second, they provide a chance for direct actionists to meet the opponents and confront the reality of what and whom they are dealing with.

IS ECONOMIC ACTION POSSIBLE?

It is pretty clear that direct action is more effective when there are economic pressures, such as boycott or strike, available. However, even if no economic tactics are available, the civil rights worker need not be discouraged. Direct action campaigns have been effective without the economic angle, for example when the Quakers struggled for religious liberty in Puritan Massachusetts. Despite much brutality and some Quaker deaths, the Puritans finally came around.

CAN A CONSTRUCTIVE PROGRAM BE DEVISED?

An activity which is useful for many direct action campaigns is the "constructive program." The Freedom School is one kind, the work camp another. These programs are helpful because (a) they draw help from people who would not engage in direct action tactics; (b) they develop organizational know-how and group spirit in new people; (c) they provide a morale boost during a time when the direct action campaign may be suffering reverses; (d) they contradict one of the prejudices whites have about "lazy Negroes who don't help themselves"; (e) they get things done which need doing. Work camps can, for example, fix up the apartments of old people, clean up vacant lots for playground space, and fix up buildings and church rooms to be used for recreational and meeting purposes. Some aspects of such a program may involve direct action, such as dumping the refuse from the vacant lot in front of the city recreational department. This draws attention to the city's failure to do the job which citizens have now taken on themselves.

HOW DO YOU CHOOSE A STRATEGY?

At some time you must decide which of a variety of possible targets you will move in on. Shall it be lunch counters or movies, churches or beaches, jobs or voting? How does one make a choice of strategy? The previous six points have outlined some of the factors which go into such a decision—basically, a consideration of these factors should give you an idea of your strengths and weaknesses. But a strategy cannot be based only on a realistic view of your strength and the opponent's condition. It must also be based on at least two other factors: the national picture and local needs. If, this year, the national thrust of the entire civil rights movement is on voter registration and political action, you would not want to divert your local movement and hence weaken this national effort. At the same time, the strategy which you choose must meet some local needs, must fill some local demand, otherwise the community will not be motivated to join in the struggle.

HOW DO YOU ESTABLISH ROOTS IN THE COMMUNITY?

Once, partly through your contacts with the community, you have determined a likely strategy, you must face the issue of the why and how of building a "grass-roots" movement in the community.

Initially, your "program" should be built only on close contact in the community—you have talked to tenants about housing, workers about employment, housewives about discriminatory pricing; you have listened for hours, in your door-to-door informal interviewing, to specific complaints about traffic lights, late public assistance payments, police brutality to a relative or friend. And through these specific complaints you have listened for a deeper, second strain of complaints common to many people, around which a community movement can be built.

Now you and your "team" (hopefully a part of the community because you live there all the time and share the life of the neighborhood) can begin to build community organizations to do the jobs which need to be done, the jobs which have come from the specific and deeper complaints of your neighbors. This turns you and your team into a political force, for you are now organizing the community to do for itself what it formerly received as favors from the white power structure, from the old wardheeler political favor-doers. These were favors exchanged for votes, or for staying in line. Now the community can gain for itself what it rightfully should have —and owe no one for favors. It is politically independent for the first time, through its own efforts spearheaded by you and your team.

In this effort, too, you have allies in and around the Negro community. First, you must become aware of the existing social service agencies and what they can and cannot do for you. Many of these may simply be agents of the power structure, but others, while incapable up to now of helping the community, can be moved by the community to lend real assistance. In a sense, many community workers in the established agencies would like to be pressured by the people so that they could pressure those above them into allocating funds and personnel for meaningful work, instead of the usual "drop-in-the-bucket" welfare plan.

Second, there are the ministers, especially important in the South when it comes to key people in the Negro community. It becomes crucial, when the ministers do not move themselves, to move their congregations, important vestrymen, etc., in order to move the ministers indirectly. For when the congregation moves, the minister finds he must move as well, or the congregation will move right out of the church. Women in key church committee positions are especially significant in this job.

Third are the many other elements which are important to the structure and organization of the community. It must be kept in mind that the working class community, Negro or white, is not "disorganized," as some social scientists say. It is well organized, but along different lines from those of other communities. The team worker must be alert to the organizational significance of "rooming houses" as well as churches, bars as well as social agencies, and gang leaders as well as community "leaders." Keen observation of the neighborhood and its habits, what it considers good and its taboos, is the first requirement of a successful grass-roots organizer.

Civil rights organizers are now making a real effort to work on a neighborhood basis. They do this because real roots in the community can only be established by means of going to work on people's everyday problems. Only in this way can large numbers of Negroes be brought into active participation in civil rights movements. In the long run, too, the process of having civil rights groups organize the Negro community may serve to undermine and eventually do away with the traditional rule of the political machine. When the civil rights organization moves into the neighborhood, it teaches citizens how to take care of their own problems without the middleman.

This new focus of activity for civil rights workers does not represent a break with nonviolent direct action; rather, it creates opportunities to use direct action in new and imaginative ways.

Little has been written about this kind of community organization problem, but those who intend to get into neighborhood work should consult some of the standard social work texts for general background information. Silberman's *Crisis in Black and White* (especially Chapter 10), Alinsky's *Reveille for Radicals,* Presthus' *Men at the Top,* and, for organizing the "mids," Seeley, Sim, and Loosley's *Crestwood Heights* are also valuable.

A word of caution in this connection: as civil rights groups such as the ministerial associations, CORE, etc., move into community work, there is a good chance that their efforts will concentrate on job training, nursery schools, literacy campaigns, etc., to such an extent that their orginal aims to secure social change will be diverted. Especially with official backing for "poverty programs," community workers will find it tempting to become a part of the powerful financial structure of "welfarism." Obviously we are not opposed to welfare. On the other hand, we would urge that civil rights direct action groups remember *why* they are engaged in community activity: to build a force for social change, for an integrated and human society. It is important not to let the *means* become an end in itself, not to lose sight of the ultimate goals of the struggle.

3 / INTERGROUP RELATIONS*

Participants in direct action, as well as other interested citizens, should be familiar with a wide range of community and state-level institutions not normally associated with "nonviolent direct action." This is particularly true in that many readers of this *Manual* are not prepared to engage in direct action, yet want to know what kinds of activities are appropriate for them in their attempts to secure "fair play" for American minority groups.

Action toward desegregation and integration apart from direct action usually involves either the enforcement of law, and/or the formation of organizations generally termed "intergroup relations organizations." All groups involved in civil rights are by definition involved with intergroup relations. But the more traditional emphasis of the intergroup relations field has been

* Much of the material in this chapter is based on John P. Dean and Alex Rosen's *A Manual of Intergroup Relations*, Chicago, Phoenix Books, 1963; Lewis Killian and Charles Grigg's *Racial Crisis in America*, New York, Prentice-Hall, 1964; George Schermer's *Guidelines: A Manual for Bi-Racial Committees*, New York, Anti-Defamation League of B'nai B'rith, 1964; and *Fair Housing Handbook*, published by the American Friends Service Committee and the National Committee Against Discrimination in Housing, 1964.

upon dealing with the power structure of a community and getting it to work out desegregation problems through mediation and negotiation with its more reluctant partners. The emphasis of the direct action groups is to place pressure upon the power structure by means of positive social dislocation, that is, by economic, political, and moral leverage. Direct action groups do engage in negotiation, but their efforts are less an attempt to get an agreement within the power structure as to how to deal with the situation, and more toward confronting the whole power structure with a conflict situation with which it must somehow come to terms.

Frequently the more traditionally oriented intergroup relations organizations see their role as that of a liaison between the civil rights groups and local groups which are resisting change. They often believe that so long as channels of communication between opposing forces can be kept open, and misunderstanding avoided, a solution to the conflict can be worked out. While direct action organizations seek to involve themselves directly as interested parties to negotiations, the traditional groups are more concerned with bringing about a better situation in the community, with or without the presence of the civil rights groups in the final settlement. In fact, sometimes the boast has been made that in a particular community, desegregation of some facility has been accomplished without pressure from a civil rights group, or, if such a group exists, without that group having had anything to do with the outcome.

We would be pulling our punches if we were merely to say that this approach is one of several and equally valid with the others. The emphasis of this *Manual* is upon direct action, and upon an assumption about community relations which says that power structures are basically conservative and opposed to social change. Direct action is intended to bring counter-power to bear, forcing change through peaceful conflict. Nonviolent direct action means, among other things, that when conflict becomes violent, those who intend to bring about a change will respond without violence, but will also keep up the pressure. This will tend to make for a more far-reaching and realistic *solution* to the conflict situation, rather than a mere postponement, or controlling, of the conflict.

Direct action groups welcome negotiation, and welcome the existence of the traditional intergroup relations organizations. But they are frequently skeptical of the efforts of such groups, because too often their existence has been a cover-up for the impression that something is being done, while nothing is really changing.

On the other hand, many IRO's have in fact made real gains for minorities, and such efforts should be carefully studied and evaluated, and of course welcomed. As with so many American institutions, they vary from place to place, and it is hard to generalize.

A number of IRO's are nationwide, well known, and have long-established reputations for their work (frequently carried out despite great risks). Several examples are the American Friends Service Committee, the Anti-Defamation League of B'nai B'rith, the American Civil Liberties Union (not strictly an IRO, but in the South nearly so), the Southern Regional Council, various "Y" groups, and innumerable church groups such as the Department of Racial and Cultural Relations, Division of Christian Life and Work, of the National Council of Churches. There are many, many others.

HUMAN RELATIONS COMMISSIONS STEP IN

IRO's which have received a great deal of attention, especially on the local level, involve the concept of the Interracial Relations or Human Relations Committee or Commission. These may be official (set up informally by a mayor or governor, or formally by local ordinance or state law) or non-official (set up solely through the efforts of private citizens, sometimes including public officials acting personally, often including representatives of civil rights groups, and occasionally functioning *as* a civil rights group when no other group locally is fighting for better conditions). HRC's may be composed either of appointed or volunteer individuals, or of delegates sent by various organizations. They are sometimes called "Mayor's Friendly Relations

Committees," "Fellowship Commissions," and the like. They almost always include some representatives of some segment of the local power structure, although perhaps not the dominant segment. Likewise, they almost always include some members of the minority group, although again not always representative of the new currents moving in the minority community. Uncle Toms, status seekers, and perpetual "official spokesmen" all too frequently populate certain HRC's.

There are several sub-categories of HRC's which deserve separate attention: (1) voluntary citizens' groups devoted to a particular community issue, such as the rapidly developing "Fair Housing Councils" in some Northern suburbs; (2) interfaith and interracial Ministerial Councils; (3) interfaith Negro Ministers' Associations; (4) frequently all-white citizens groups devoted primarily to law and order (rather than to desegregation), but in which desegregation becomes a by-product (for example, SOS—Save Our Schools, Inc., in New Orleans, and OASIS— Organizations Assisting Schools in September, in Atlanta); (5) Chamber of Commerce and other businessmen's groups which sometimes take on the job of HRC's when it seems that racial "disturbances" may result in serious business losses.

An examination of HRC's can begin at the national level with the U.S. Commission on Civil Rights. It has no enforcement powers, but it can collect and publish data and make legislative recommendations. The newly established Community Relations Service has the negotiating and mediating job common to many HRC's. About twenty-six states, mostly Northern and Western, have official HRC's, twenty established by law to administer state laws against discrimination of various kinds. Many are limited to collecting data and promoting "amicable relationships among various racial and cultural groups," to quote from the Delaware law. Some have hearing and enforcement powers and can secure court orders, or can themselves issue orders requiring compliance with state laws. In general, it can be said that such HRC's are as good as the amount of power given them by law, plus the degree of willingness of the state political structure to allow them to use that power. Assuming again that political power tends to be conservative and not to push for changes, it would seem that "willingness" often depends on how much pressure the civil rights movement can mount against state-level politicians.

Local HRC's tend to work best when they are (a) official, that is, established by law; (b) have specific responsibilities under the law; (c) have enforcement power to order compliance; (d) have some prestige personnel, plus some real representation from the Negro community; (e) have an adequate budget; (f) have a paid staff; and (g) have power to act both as administrator of a law and as mediator (communicator) between conflicting parties. The HRC's fields of activity should ideally include jobs, housing, schools, voting, public accommodations, and police relations (police brutality).*

As for actual results, little can be said definitely. The community-level HRC "movement" stemmed in large part from the 1960 sit-ins in the South. Many were formed during "cooling-off" periods following demonstrations, and some were simply delaying actions on the part of local white power structures. By the summer of 1960, HRC's had been set up in some thirty cities of the upper South as the direct or indirect result of sit-in activity. But as late as 1962, only about 16.5 percent of all Southern cities of 10,000 population or more had such committees, according to Killian and Grigg's study. About one-third of those hadn't met during the year prior to the study.

On the other hand, we don't know how many of the less formal "Mayor's Committees," frequently temporary, did not show up in the study. It does seem that in many of the cities in which facilities have been integrated since February, 1960, HRC-type committees have been quite important in arranging with representatives of businesses the procedures for integrating lunch counters, restaurants, movies, etc., and in gaining agreement on such procedures. But it is also clear that without mass demonstrations or the threat of demonstrations, the committees would frequently not have been formed and negotiations toward desegregation would not have taken place.

* This paragraph is based chiefly on George Schermer's booklet, cited earlier.

CHARLOTTE: A CASE STUDY

The situation in Charlotte, North Carolina, seems to illustrate some of these points. The sit-in movement there, under the leadership of students at Johnson C. Smith University, began on February 9, 1960. In mid-March the mayor proposed a special study group on race relations (amid talk of a general boycott of downtown stores by the Negro community). This developed into the Mayor's Committee on Friendly Relations. The Mayor's Committee worked in vain on local merchants well into June. Students resumed sit-ins on June 22 after a cooling-off period, combining this with a boycott of all downtown stores. One week later merchants asked for consultation with the Mayor's Committee, and by July 4 the merchants had agreed to terms. On July 9, fifteen students were served at seven stores in the downtown area. The local HRC served the valuable function of channeling the merchants' change of position in such a way as to make it appear that it was engineered by other white forces (the Mayor's Committee), rather than by the civil rights movement. This got the merchants off the hook. But it was the students, not the committee, who made the merchants come to terms.

In the spring and summer of 1963 Charlotte "voluntarily" desegregated its leading hotels and motels, most of the rest of the downtown restaurants, and the better movie theaters. A new wave of sit-ins and other demonstrations was hitting neighboring cities. The chamber of commerce then recommended that all businesses catering to the general public open to all customers without regard to race. Members of the chamber's executive committee and board of directors met with owners and let them know how the chamber felt. Chamber officials brought Negroes to lunch or dinner in "trial" runs. The mayor, elected that spring with the Negro vote, was in on it. But again the chamber of commerce didn't come to this point without the threat of demonstrations locally and the example of social dislocation in nearby communities.

There is both a promise and a danger in this kind of situation.

The promise is that local power structures, as reflected in their governments and in their business groups, can be moved—not by good words, but by counter-power—in the direction of a better society. The danger is that if they can be moved for good by nonviolent direct action, they can also be moved for evil by other power—or they can be prevented from moving. They can even be moved for good purposes by violent means, in the short run, for the power structure is frequently unable to distinguish between violent and nonviolent dislocation, or the threat of dislocation. If we are to realize the promise inherent in this kind of a conflict situation, then we must see to it that our power is always present, organized, and ready to move.

In Jacksonville, Florida, for instance, sit-in demonstrations in August, 1960, were met with concerted resistance by Klan-type groups, after police had given indications they would not protect civil rights organizations. On August 27 of that year a race riot took place. Negroes, many of them members of juvenile gangs, went into the streets to protect their community against Klan raiding. One Negro was killed. The white community, united to preserve segregation, was prepared to permit violence and dislocation of business. Despite a call by white clergymen to organize an official interracial committee, the mayor refused.

Four years later the same mayor had still failed to form an official HRC, although a private citizens group did exist. A three-day riot by Negroes took place on March 23-25, 1964, and a Negro woman was shot to death. But this was primarily an intra-racial riot and did not involve white citizens. On March 25 the mayor called for an "unofficial" biracial committee, to be led by segments of the city's business leadership. Three days of Negro rioting finally seemed to accomplish what four years of nonviolent demonstration and patient negotiation could not accomplish. Small wonder, given this kind of reluctance to move, that nationalist groups are able to get a hearing among the more bitter and frustrated elements of the Negro community.*

* The information concerning Charlotte in 1963 and Jacksonville in 1964 is based on Pat Watters' *Charlotte,* a Special Report of the Southern Regional Council (May, 1964), and on the S.R.C.'s Report L-47, "The Question From Jacksonville," dated April 16, 1964. Memphis and Louisville data which follow are based on special reports prepared for the S.R.C. by Benjamin Muse in 1964.

HRC's operating in the upper South and in border states appear to be able to obtain better results, given the greater willingness of the local power structure to permit Negroes a share in the economy and in local politics. Even in deep Southern Memphis, a volunteer, non-official Memphis Committee on Community Relations has been able, with much behind-the-scenes work, to open up some Negro job opportunities and, backed up by extensive sit-ins and other demonstrations, to help in ridding the city of many flagrant racial barriers. In Louisville, a city ordinance established a Louisville Human Relations Commission in March, 1962. It recommended local legislation against discriminatory practices, and an ordinance was adopted in May, 1963. This was a major change from 1960, when the city board of aldermen rejected both the establishment of an HRC and all attempts to legislate on the subject of public accommodations. But again, the change was backed up, if not initiated, by waves of sit-in demonstrations in 1960 and 1961. A series of demonstrations in 1961, which took place almost daily for several weeks and which involved about 1,000 arrests, succeeded in desegregating some 200 downtown restaurants and lunch counters even before the formation of the official HRC, although an earlier "Mayor's Advisory Committee" had been set up by that time.

While it is difficult to make an overall statement about the success of HRC's in the North (particularly since the failures tend to draw more public attention than the successes), success does seem to depend on no political interference by the local and state power structures, as well as on the leverage applied by civil rights groups. There seems to be more progress in non-election years, when politicians feel they do not risk their jobs by upholding the letter and spirit of the law. In both Philadelphia and Chester, Pennsylvania, for example, local HRC's were bypassed or rendered at least temporarily ineffective during racial demonstrations in 1963 and 1964, because local political considerations took priority. As a result, in both places direct action groups view the HRC's as simple appendages to the local power structure, that is, as window-dressing.

GOOD NEIGHBORS ORGANIZE

Citizens' groups which overlap direct action, but do not emphasize it, include Fair Housing Councils. These can be organized for one or both of two purposes: (1) to help integrate a neighborhood, previously all-white, without violence and in the best spirit of harmony; and (2) to maintain the integrated character of a neighborhood or block in the face of a potential "runaway" by white residents as the result of panic selling.

The "Good Neighbor Pledge"-signing campaign is a feature of either purpose. This is a way of finding out who is sympathetic, and of putting neighbors on record for fair play in housing.

Once a Fair Housing Council is organized (frequently with the assistance of prominent local people) it becomes necessary to set up a series of committees, composed of neighbors, to take care of such jobs as informing members of the legal and business aspects of the housing market, setting up a speakers' bureau, and locating resource people who are experts on various aspects of race relations and public relations. The FHC concerned with integrating a neighborhood will need first to locate houses and apartments available on an "open-occupancy" basis. This may involve negotiations and perhaps even direct action aimed at real estate firms, sometimes backed up by legal measures.

The FHC will also have to find prospective renters and buyers, and help them through the ropes of obtaining appropriate housing. If housing is denied them, members of the FHC will want to *test* (that is, send whites to try to rent or purchase the same housing). Negotiations and direct action may follow.

"Operation Window-Shop," also called "walk-ins," may be a project of an FHC at any time. This involves testing available housing, especially newly opened developments, periodically. This is done by sending white, then Negro, then white couples to the unit available for rent or sale in order to find out if there is any difference in treatment.

Members of the FHC should be alert to possible trouble in the community as the result of a "move-in." If the minority-group family (this is by no means only a Negro problem) wishes it, members of the FHC should be on hand on the day of the move. Appropriate government agencies, including police, should be contacted if trouble is expected. It is wisest, under such circumstances, to move in on a weekday, during the day, so that large numbers of neighbors are not available to mill around and start trouble. Friendly neighbors should be alerted, and clergymen should be asked to visit their parishioners in the area in advance, and possibly to be on hand. Members of the FHC should be prepared, in case of really big trouble, to do extensive educational work in the community, to stay with the family (possibly sleeping in the home) over a longer period, and to face violence from mob action if police fail in their duty. Workshops on nonviolence are a good practice if such a situation is expected.

The chief task of FHC's in neighborhoods where members of minority groups are moving in, and where there is a risk that the neighborhood will become "reverse segregated" because of whites moving out, is to prevent panic selling. Panic selling is frequently promoted by real estate interests on the theory that, in order to avoid living in the block with the minority group, people will sell at a sacrifice. The price then goes back up— and more—and minority group members must pay inflated prices because of a general shortage of housing available to them on an "open-occupancy" basis. The key to preventing panic selling is organizing the neighborhood and persuading neighbors to stay. Neighbors may be willing to post THIS HOUSE NOT FOR SALE signs to discourage real estate men and encourage each other. Information about the actual economic and social results of having members of minority groups in a block, based on the experience of other parts of the city and country, may help.

Ultimately, of course, it is only when all members of minority groups are able to have full access to decent jobs and schools that all "risk" will be eliminated. Until that time, some people will always be able to find some reason to leave a neighborhood because they fear an influx of people with lower incomes and educational levels. In the long run, therefore, FHC's, in order to be fully effective, will have to come to grips with the broader issues of housing, jobs, and education beyond the borders of their own communities.

HOW CAN "LEADERS" LEAD?

Community leaders, no matter where they are, have an important role to play in race relations. Clear-cut and positively stated policy on critical matters early in a community conflict situation may prevent the problem from getting out of hand. Naturally, there is always a risk, particularly in the deep South (although by no means exclusively so), that the man who takes a clear-cut stand, whether based on his conscience or on his pocketbook, will be isolated and smeared. Nevertheless, a failure to provide positive leadership is often responsible for a deteriorated situation even where at one time there was little danger. Private business leaders, especially from companies which are just setting themselves up in a community (and hence have no set pattern or way of doing things yet), can move beyond what is locally accepted in the way of minority-group relations. This may include taking steps to recruit Negroes to jobs not previously held by non-whites, in order to help close the gap between Negro and white living conditions in this community. (One technique here is to hire Negro personnel men.)

Ministers, too, have an important job in backing up "fair play." The many church-sponsored statements in support of the student nonviolent movement in 1960 were extremely significant in getting this movement accepted as legitimate, despite the fact that laws were being violated in the course of civil disobedience. White ministers on the picket line were a crucial element in the settlement of the 1960 sit-ins in Charlotte, North Carolina, for example.

All-Negro ministerial associations frequently have a great deal of potential power in a community. In Philadelphia, an informally organized group of four hundred Negro ministers, by means of a "selective patronage program" (a boycott), broke discriminatory hiring practices in a number of important businesses. In a manner not known even to the local HRC, the ministers chose a company which they believed to be discriminating in some way. Then delegations of four or five ministers visited the company to talk things over. Failing results, definite demands for certain numbers of jobs at certain levels (usually including white collar) were made. Utilizing four hundred pulpits and contacts with the NAACP, the Negro press, Negro Masonic lodges, and other groups, "selective patronage" was then urged. Following a two-month boycott against the Tasty Baking Company in the summer of 1960, demands to hire two Negro drivers, two clerical workers, and several girls in the icing department were met. A similar boycott against the Pepsi-Cola Company lasted just two weeks before similar demands were met; a boycott against Gulf Oil lasted just one week. Many companies gave in before a boycott was needed—within four years the Negro group succeeded in opening some three hundred jobs which had been all-white before that time.

However, with a minimum of some 27,000 Negroes unemployed in the city (twice the unemployment *rate* of whites), and with many companies laying off their *white* help, the efforts of the ministers still proved to be minute. Furthermore, the efforts resulted in a good deal of hostility from the white working class community, which feared for its jobs. Eventually the ministers' group moved into the field of job training and retraining, and today plays an important role as sponsor of several federally supported "poverty program" youth training centers.

In the South, many people who would find themselves too vulnerable were they to speak out directly on the race issue can still work through "law and order" groups such as SOS. These groups are often supported by elements of the business community, chambers of commerce, ministerial associations, etc., even though they are working indirectly for better conditions for minority groups, because that is not itself the issue. SOS and similar groups do work for a changed situation, though the presumed reason for the change is to avoid violence and public disorder—either on the part of civil rights groups (who will demonstrate if they don't get a change), or on the part of segregationist groups (who will act if the change is forthcoming).

The SOS-type group holds that the change (usually one sanc-
tioned by law, or even required by law) is cheaper than stand-
ing still, that obedience to a new law (even though disagree-
able) is preferable to illegality. Even here, however, we are
talking about groups which would not have appeared without
some kind of threat or leverage from some side in a conflict
situation. Nowhere does change seem to occur willingly, without pressure, without the exertion of some power by someone
or some group.

That pressure must be planned and it must be organized.
Appeals based on "good will" and "fair play" alone do not work.
Appeals must be backed up with the leverage of actual people
prepared to organize, to sacrifice, and to take sides in a community conflict situation.

4 / SETTING UP AN ORGANIZATION

Once the civil rights worker has analyzed the community and thought about a strategy, he should proceed to set up an organization. Forms of organization, their structures, and their affiliations if any will depend on the job decided on and the personnel available. The worker may want to join an existing group in order to influence it; he may want to set up an ad hoc or temporary group composed either of individuals or of representatives of other groups; or he may want to create a new group. In recent years most groups tend to be "single-cause" rather than many-purpose, with the exception of some student groups (in some cases, single-cause groups later develop into many-purpose groups). It is generally easier to join an existing group than to set up a new one, and to affiliate rather than to maintain complete independence. There are certain advantages stemming from national affiliation, including financial help, staff help, legal aid, reputation, and aid in moving against concerns and politicians with far-off headquarters in other cities and states.

Organization implies bureaucracy. Every organization has bureaucracy, and this is not necessarily a "dirty" word. It simply means that there is a chain of command or communication through which decisions are carried out. Bureaucracy becomes "dirty" only when decision-making no longer reflects the rank and file membership, and/or when the structure interferes with making decisions. This happens when the structure becomes too large, or when decision-making processes are unclear so that decisiveness is lacking, or when routine alone becomes central in the life of the organization.

Every organization, whether it is the U.S. Army, a business corporation, or a peace or civil rights group, must have a chain of command. Our assumption is that the chain of command should go from the bottom up, that is, should be democratic. This is so because democracy is (a) efficient, more so than dictatorship in the long run; (b) better able to move in the direction of creating a more human society, because it involves people in the determination of their own destinies, hence in the fuller involvement and development of their personalities; and (c) more able to recruit the kind of forces needed really to overcome oppression and injustice, because in the long run movements based on demagogy do not result in justice—the means help to determine the ends.

There are ways in which democratic decision-making and full participation by the rank-and-file can be undercut. Early in the formation of a group a decision must be made as to structure, and while democratic structure does not guarantee democracy, it does help. A decision must also be made on how decisions are to be taken: by parliamentary or by consensus (the Quaker "sense of the meeting") methods. Both have advantages, and both have disadvantages. Consensus tends to work best when the members of the group have basic agreement on philosophy, while the parliamentary system tends to guarantee representation to organized minorities and recognizes the importance of caucuses. Both systems can be manipulated by persons with the best intentions, not to speak of those with less than the highest moral outlook.

Several kinds of conditions help to undermine democracy aside from outright manipulation, or help make manipulation possible. Wearing the group out with late and boring meetings, or holding the group until most members have gone, leaves the way open for a well-organized minority to railroad ideas through. Having present officers appoint or elect other officers should generally be regarded with suspicion. Nominating committees for officers, rather than nominations from the floor, are another technique for keeping decision-making within a small group. Most important of all is the development of informal person-to-person relationships: shortcuts, doing favors, and the praiseworthy but misdirected desire to want to avoid mistakes—hence letting "experts" do all the jobs. This tends to happen partic-

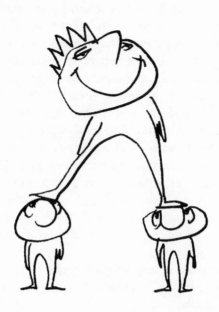

ularly in the midst of crises and emergencies when "we can't afford to make mistakes," and can't take a chance on letting an untrained person do a job and learn at the risk of having him make mistakes. Unless deliberate decisions are made by the group to expand the techniques of the trade, those techniques (such as running a meeting, writing a leaflet, running a mimeo machine, being picket captain, etc.) will remain the property of a few "experts," who tend gradually, and frequently without realizing it, to exclude the rank-and-file members from a real role in the organization.

In civil rights groups conditions of crisis always exist. This makes the situation more serious. In addition, you will run into the argument that decision-making should be limited to those who participate fully in organizational work—something that is not possible for everyone, given the speed of the movement and the constant meetings required. A second-class membership can develop under such circumstances, and a type of clique arises in which the "true revolutionaries," that is, those whose *entire* lives are taken up with the movement, have a different life from the rest of the members, different values, slang, etc. Insofar as such a clique criticizes current values it may have a contribution to make, but when it separates itself from its own rank-and-file, and from the community at large, because of its style of living, it does the movement a disservice. Democracy suffers.

If you need to fight against the growth of non-democratic tendencies in an organization, you must organize your action (that is, form caucuses). This is true whether the non-democratic group is informal, or whether a clearly anti-democratic faction exists. You must organize pro-democratic people to conduct a clear-cut fight on this issue; otherwise, after a time, the organization is doomed to develop in such a way as to undermine its ultimate goals: the democratic and just development of society.

Whether you are conducting a struggle within your own organization or working as a democratic minority in another group, several suggestions may help:

(1) All organizations have three primary functions: policy-making, organization, and education (including both education of the group itself and public relations). Regardless of what body makes policy (conventions, executive committees, etc.) he who is in charge of carrying out policy ultimately determines what happens. The organizer, secretary, coordinator of committees, administrator is the man to watch—or the man to be. This fact can be used either for evil or for good.

(2) You must organize your group into a caucus, meet ahead of meetings, plan strategy, and have a floor leader. Sit in scattered positions throughout the audience. Save your best speaker for last in an exchange from the floor. Know your parliamentary procedure so as not to be outmaneuvered, and to make best use of your numbers.

(3) Remember that you, as a leader, are no good without an organized following, just as an officer is no good without a top-notch first sergeant. The good leader must have a *perspective* (not constantly react to situations only as they arise), *credibility* (not promise what cannot be accomplished, not over- or under-

shoot the potential, but keep the group moving at its capacity), and "image" or *personality*. Remember that a leader can be cut down just as surely by apathy as by elections, and that you can sabotage any organization by obeying *all* the rules carefully, just as you can sabotage it by a "slow-down." This, after all, is just another kind of "passive resistance."

(4) The good leader recognizes minority points of view without being bullied by them. Dissenters are a part of the movement unless proven otherwise, and above all they are human beings and must be treated as such. A good leader will insist that arguments be to the point and will not allow "ad hominem" or name-calling arguments which attempt to discredit people's thinking by some form of "guilt by association."

JOBS THAT NEED DOING

The above are general points. What are some of the specific jobs that need doing? *

(1) Once the executive committee and the officers have been set up (with clearly established lines of authority, responsibility, and decision-making, and with as little overlap as possible) we are ready to move.

(2) A timetable for action is worthwhile. Persons who have charge of such jobs as publicity, office management, transportation, communication, housing, training, supplies, finances, and literature should be appointed or elected. Special resource persons, when needed, should be lined up: workshop leaders, legal counsel, public relations specialists, etc.

(3) Frequently a headquarters in the field must be set up. Select its location carefully for convenience and possible symbolic value. Keep quarters neat and clean. Your headquarters speaks for you; you will want to post notices and posters and possibly open it with a reception and press conference.

(4) Finances are always a tricky matter. Open a special bank account if necessary. Be clear on any tax-exemption problems. Set up a simple bookkeeping system in case your regular book-

---

* This section is based partly on Charles Walker, *Organizing for Nonviolent Direct Action*, Cheyney, Pennsylvania, 1961.

keeper is arrested. Your opponents will seek excuses to charge misuse of funds and there may be investigations. Your financial affairs should be kept fanatically clean.

(5) Office supplies, communications equipment (walkie-talkies, etc.), and equipment for meetings must be on hand when they are needed. Make sure your machinery is kept in good repair so that it can function when you need it. The problem of record keeping must be clarified: while you may not wish to have records seized (hence have supporters punished), at the same time it is important to keep track of activities for the sake of accounting for responsibilities, informing new personnel of work in progress when they take over, and helping sociologists and historians in their job for the future.

(6) Secrecy: It is possible to confuse and delay the obtaining of "secret" information by your opponents in various ways. However, if your opponents are determined, this is pointless. It results in *inefficiency* because you have to cover up much that you do from your own members, *authoritarianism* because you cannot tell your members what is going on, and *mistrust*. In any case your opponents, if they are determined, will plant "informers" and/or modern electronic devices in such a way that your activities will be an open book. You may as well open the book and be fully honest about your plans to begin with. You should try to plan tactics (to be discussed later) which do not depend on secrecy for their value.

(7) Register or have records of participants in all projects wherever possible (a) in order to keep them informed prior to the event; (b) to find out if they have special skills; (c) to keep track of problems as they develop; (d) to follow up later for deeper involvement; (e) to inform attorneys or relatives in case of arrest, accident, or violence. Participants in long-term projects should be insured, if possible.

(8) Participation in a project or membership in an organization should be conditioned upon acceptance of a written discipline, or upon some set of principles or constitution. No exceptions should be made. It is your job to educate people to the acceptance of your principles, but until they do, they should

stay out. Such principles do not have to be complicated or numerous. In this way you can cut down on misunderstandings and violations of lines of responsibility and authority, and thus limit the likelihood of violence because of your own people losing control of a demonstration or of themselves. This also helps the morale and public image of the movement, and gives outsiders a sense that the organization is something special to which it is a privilege to belong.

(9) Relations between persons in the group (also to be discussed in Chapter 6) will always be a problem. Boy-girl situations develop. Rules rarely work, so none will be given here. Sloppy public demonstrations of personal affection, needless to say, violate other aspects of most disciplines, and can be handled that way. Sloppy clothing likewise.

(10) Psychological problems also arise. People join movements for all kinds of reasons, and the untrained person will rarely be able to distinguish "real" from stated reasons except in extreme cases. This does not need to become an issue until personal problems interfere with the working of the group. If at all possible, a somewhat older person with experience in family situations should have a kind of leading role in the organization so that he can step in and offer guidance without appearing to interfere in anybody's personal life or making the problem person feel pushed around.

(11) The white participant in civil rights activities, especially (although not exclusively) in the deep South, faces a special problem: how to communicate and live with Negroes in a movement which is primarily of, by, and for Negroes, and how to survive in action. To varying degrees he may be treated as a second-class participant by Negroes, and frequently, though in very subtle ways, he will be called upon to "prove" his sincerity. This is a difficult role. On the one hand, the white participant should not give in to reverse racism in order to be accepted—he should be accepted because of what he does, and not because of what he is. On the other hand, he must establish contact and communication and maintain them in order to be effective. The white participant should not be afraid to take on

an equal role, including a part in the decision-making process, but he should try to establish his credentials as one who has the right to participate because he, too, has put himself on the "firing line." The white participant has many of the problems which face an anthropologist or a sociologist visiting a group with which he is unfamiliar. To be accepted without losing one's own individuality and standards is not easy.

PUBLIC RELATIONS

You should not assume that because our cause is just, anyone who is worthwhile will support it—or that anyone who does not support us isn't worth trying to get. Prejudices run deep and must be dealt with. Allies are essential, because (a) civil rights workers are a very small minority in this country and cannot carry enough weight to change society no matter how moral the cause; and (b) certain kinds of allies are important because they lead to the breakdown of significant points of resistance (e.g., ministers, scholars, dignified mothers of white governors). It is therefore important, while not compromising, to try to limit the amount of antagonism from potential allies. This is the key to good "public relations." It involves primarily two things: cutting down on actions which can be misinterpreted to be hostile and negative; and improving the interpretation of all activities. Remember that many people are only looking for an excuse *not* to support the movement. While we cannot avoid creating excuses for those who are really looking for them, we can avoid presenting them on a silver platter.

What we mean when we say "public relations" is really "propaganda." Propaganda, like bureaucracy, is not necessarily a dirty word. It has become dirty because propaganda has come to be associated with lying and distortion of the truth. The distinction is often made between propaganda (which has a distinct message) and education (which leaves conclusions open). But even education is propaganda, because leaving conclusions open is a kind of message, or value, in the direction of democracy.

Before any educational or propaganda campaign is begun it is important to sit down and analyze your "target population," the people whom you want to move (or in some cases keep in their present state of mind in the face of campaigns by others to move them—propaganda is sometimes defensive). There is, first of all, the hard core of supporters (refer to Chapter 2, the section dealing with *Who Are Your Friends, and Who Are Your Opponents?*). Then there are friends whom you want to bring in closer. Then there is the vast neutral public. Then there are those in opposition, in various degrees, to the cause. The final objective of all propaganda is to move everyone one step closer to you, or, in cases where there is an offensive against you, to have them not move away from you. Every propaganda item (mass meetings, press releases, leaflets, TV programs, etc.) should be aimed at a particular segment of the population, your "target."

Various publicity methods which you may want to consider include: background information sheets to support press releases for newsmen and community leaders; brief biographical sketches of well-known leaders and participants for "human interest" stories; press releases for dailies, the wire services, special press services (religious, labor, Negro, etc.), neighborhood papers, radio and TV news departments, and commentators and columnists who are sympathetic. You may want to offer advance interviews or tape record special speeches. By all means try to visit key editors, news directors, and special reporters in order to interpret events. Writing letters to the editor should not be neglected, but they should be kept short and to the point.

It is crucial to remember that your job is to inform, not to seek publicity for publicity's sake. Try not to be put into the position of doing things for the press which are not a natural part of the action, no matter how picturesque they may be, but remember to be friendly in your replies to the press, and try to interpret what you do as fully as possible.

When you are speaking "on the record" you should be particularly careful to quote accurately and give only facts of which you are certain. Double-checking is more important than being fast with an answer. If you are the public affairs officer, you should try to do plenty of reading on this complex subject.

Press releases should be clearly marked as to time of release, and should be double-spaced. They should not be too long—two pages at maximum. After a while you will get to know the peculiarities of the local press and you will tailor your releases to meet their requirements of format. All press releases should read like a news story, beginning in the first sentence or two (at most) with Who, What, Where, When, and Why:

> Joe Brotherhood (WHO), chairman of the local chapter of Citizens for Equal Rights, this morning (WHEN) announced a full-scale boycott (WHAT) of all major downtown department stores (WHERE) by Negro citizens. He said the "no-buy" campaign would remain in effect until all the stores hire a satisfactory number of Negro clerks (WHY).
>
> Brotherhood, 32, who is theology professor at nearby Baptist Seminary, said he had the agreement of four Negro churches and five Negro community groups on the ban. (etc.)

Here are some general cautions for publicity campaigns, leaflets, and other affairs of a public relations nature:

(1) Keep leaflets readable. Dont clutter them up with too much reading material. Start out with something that will hold the reader's attention—"Police Brutality in This Neighborhood," not "Citizens for Equal Rights."

(2) Keep your public relations down to earth. Make your charges believable. Ask people to do something they can really do right now, given their present state of mind. "Come to Freedom School," not "Go Immediately to Register." Don't insult their basic prejudices or beliefs. You want to communicate, not drive them away (e.g., don't say "your preachers are nothing but Uncle Toms." It's libelous, anyway, to charge a person publicly with being a Communist, or an Uncle Tom!)

(3) Don't promise what you can't deliver. People who disagree with your ideas may gradually come to believe in you as a person if you really show you can deliver. Try small things first. Don't try too much, because failure tends to undermine morale.

(4) Watch your language. Use the English that makes sense to the community in which you are working. Watch your appearance. Appearance is a communicating device. You cannot expect people to raise their own standards of cleanliness, or look up to you as a leader, if you act like a slob. The civil rights worker gives up some of his private rights when he joins the movement.

(5) Keep social affairs social. Don't push too hard on newcomers. Be friendly and make them feel at home. Don't huddle in a corner with the in-group clique. Don't acquire the reputation of having absolutely fixed views, of being dogmatic and inflexible. When in doubt, shake hands.

CONDUCTING A MEETING

It is pointless to try to write a guide to parliamentary procedure in a manual like this. Every organization, over a period of time, develops its own procedures, somewhat based on the parliamentary rules laid down in *Roberts Rules of Order,* but modified to meet specific local conditions. The most important thing to remember about procedure is that its chief purpose is to get business conducted efficiently while protecting the will of the majority and the rights of the minority. Procedures should be amended, changed, thrown out, and invented as long as that chief purpose can get accomplished better.

A typical business *agenda* might read as follows:

(1) *Call* the meeting *to order:* "The meeting will please come to order."

(2) Have the secretary read the *minutes* of the previous meeting, with emphasis on the main points, motions passed, and action approved. Ask, "Are there any corrections to the minutes?" Then, after all corrections are made, "The minutes stand approved as corrected." Some organizations like to have the rest of the agenda read at this point, with specific topics listed, so that members may know what is ahead.

(3) Have the secretary read short summaries of the more important *correspondence,* especially letters from the national office. If action is required, it should be taken either at this point or under old or new business.

(4) *Reports* of special officers (treasurer, particularly, plus membership committee chairman, etc.) and committees (such as the executive committee, special projects committee, housing, education, public accommodations, etc.). After each report, ask for questions or discussion from the floor. There may be motions asking specific action or correcting the actions reported on at this time.

(5) Unfinished, or *old business* should be taken care of next. This is business which has not been covered by committee reports. Ask the floor, "Is there any unfinished business to come before the body?"

(6) *New business* should be next on the agenda. Some new business may have been reported by a committee, such as the executive committee, and this committee may wish to make a more formal report at this point and ask for action. When this is concluded ask, "Is there further new business?"

(7) Some organizations have a place on the agenda for *"Good and Welfare,"* meaning more general gripes. This is a good place to air them and try to cope with such problems out in the open.

(8) "There being no further business, the chair will entertain a motion to *adjourn.*"

Before and after many meetings in the civil rights field there may be a short prayer, a moment of silence for meditation, or a short song.

While there is little point in outlining a formal method of procedure, there are some keys to having an orderly meeting: *

(1) Before starting a meeting, the chairman should be sure that he has an outline of the business to be considered (the agenda).

(2) Any time an officer or a committee makes a report, there should be a motion to accept or adopt it, or change it, or, sometimes, reject it.

(3) The chairman should always state clearly the motion on which the vote is about to be taken in order that everyone has

---

* These are based on *A Call to Order,* a guide to parliamentary procedure prepared by the United States National Student Association.

a clear understanding of the issue. Amendments are usually in order after a motion has been made, and they are voted on before the main motion.

(4) Courtesy to the group is the key to an orderly meeting. Every member has rights equal to every other member.

(5) Only one subject at a time should claim the attention of the group.

(6) The will of the majority must be carried out, and the rights of the minority must be preserved.

Sometimes this can be done better through "participatory" rather than parliamentary processes. Oppenheimer's pamphlet, "Alienation or Participation," available from Students for a Democratic Society, deals with this more extensively.

5 / CITIZENSHIP AND VOTER REGISTRATION*

In much of the South repression is the law, oppression a way of life, and veering from the path of "our way of life" is not tolerated at all. Here an independent idea is subversion that must be squelched, for each bit of intellectual initiative represents a threat. Negroes have learned what is necessary for immediate survival: silence is safest, so volunteer nothing and tell "them" only what they want to hear. Workers in the South will be teaching people who have lived in the South all their lives. They have been deprived of decent education, denied free expression and free thought, and most of all denied the right to question. *Your job: to help them begin to question.*

What are the people like? They are each different, but they will have in common the scars of the system. Some will be cynical. Some will be distrustful. All will have a serious lack of preparation both with regard to academic subjects and contemporary issues—but all will have a knowledge far beyond their years of how to survive in a society that is out to destroy them. Because they have this knowledge, this awareness of the extent of evil in the world, they will be ahead of you in many ways. But most of this knowledge is negative. It is only half the picture, and it is this half which is crumbling. There is great reason to hope for the first time. *Your job: to help the people see this hope and inspire them to go after it.*

What will they demand of you? They will demand that you

* This chapter is based in part on notes distributed by the Council of Federated Organizations (COFO) for teaching in Mississippi, but much of it is general enough to apply to other areas in which civil rights workers have contact with the local population for various educational purposes, including northern urban areas.

be honest. Honesty is an attitude toward life which is communicated by everything you do. Since you, too, will be in a learning situation honesty means that you will ask questions as well as answer them. It means that if you don't know something you will say so. It means that you will not "act" a part in the attempt to compensate for all they've endured in the South. You can't compensate for that, and they don't want you to try. These people have been taught by the system not to trust. You have to be trust-*worthy*. There is little you can teach them about prejudice and segregation. They know. What you can do is help them to develop ideas and associations and tools with which they can do something about segregation and prejudice.

How? The key to teaching is honesty and creativity. Materials prepared by experts can help, but ultimately you must discover the way for yourself.

In some areas you will find that you may be the first civil rights worker there, and if you are white, almost certainly you will be the first white civil rights worker. You will have to deal with the problem of your own "novelty" as well as with the educational challenge. In such areas, interest in education will have to be created, and teachers will have to recruit their students.

In other areas there have been projects in the past, and you will be warmly welcomed. Almost everywhere you can count on one thing: there is a local desire for a worker. Otherwise you would not be sent.

It is important to realize that many of the communities in which you may find yourself are in the process of rapid social change, and the program in which you are engaged will be in the midst of this ferment. You may find yourself involved in political activities—registering people to vote, organizing political rallies, campaigning for Negro candidates, and preparing to challenge the local political power structure. The classroom experience and the real life political experience, both for you and for your students, will be linked and will overlap. This is how the classroom experience will become real. At the same time you will have to balance your local participation with the need to prepare for classes.

In some communities local activity may go beyond politics, involving direct action, mass demonstrations, jail, etc. You must keep a sensitive ear to the ground so that if this should happen you can make a tactical choice to continue the educational program or possibly modify it.

Educational techniques will depart considerably from the formal classroom lecture system many students remember from college days. Since one of the prime goals is to develop local leadership, it is important to help students express themselves. Thus *discussion* is the preferred technique. Discussion helps to encourage expression, brings feelings out into the open where they can be discussed and dealt with productively, develops participation on many levels, develops group loyalty and responsibility, and develops critical and self-critical faculties, as well as the ability to take criticism from others. While short lectures, socio-drama, reading aloud, and singing can all be used, discussion should be used as a follow-up in almost all cases.

HINTS FOR BETTER TEACHING

Here are some hints for better teaching and discussion leadership:

Subject matter should always be related to the student's level of experience and his everyday problems.

No expressions of anybody's feelings should ever be ignored or passed over. Bring them out and discuss them honestly and with compassion.

The classroom atmosphere should be informal, but not sloppy. You may want to arrange seats in a circle, use first names, let the students lead occasionally, etc.

Sessions should always be prepared in advance, especially if audio-visual aids are to be used in the most effective way.

At the beginning of the session, summarize quickly what was covered the day before, or ask a student to do so. At the end of a session, summarize what was covered during the session, or let a student do so, and let the group know what will be done in the next session.

Keep the language simple, but don't talk down. At the same time, always keep standards up so that you set an example.

Hold your criticisms until a good give-and-take atmosphere has been established between you and the students. Be positive: praise accomplishments whenever possible, especially before making a criticism.

One-hour sessions are usually maximum for any single session.

The group leader should lead, not dominate; give direction and keep discussion going, not "control."

The best way to keep things moving is to ask questions, preferably the kind that can't be answered just "yes" or "no."

Encourage participation by *everyone,* without bulldozing the reluctant, quiet participant.

The good leader should be willing to answer questions at all times, and share his own experiences and feelings too.

In a situation where any verbal expression at all is a sign of progress, the leader should not be too critical and should protect students from each other's overly critical and downgrading attacks, if such should take place.

KEEPING RECORDS

If you are setting up a voter registration or citizenship project by yourself, you will have to draw up a budget. Here is a sample budget for a straight three-week voter registration project involving twenty persons plus two leaders, showing the kind of items that must be provided for.

Food	$420.00
Utilities	15.00
Household supplies	15.00
Postage, phone, office supplies	10.00
Travel on job	30.00
Truck rental	10.00
Insurance ($1.15 per person per week)	70.00
Education & recreation	30.00
Leaders' honorarium	100.00
Leaders' travel home	100.00
Total	800.00 plus travel of participants

One, but by no means the only, way to schedule citizenship workshops in a short, three-week project, is to hold three of them: (1) You and Your Vote—Why Vote? (2) How to Register. (3) Know Your Candidate. In canvassing neighborhoods for participants, as well as for people to register, it is useful to keep records, as indicated on the following sample "Daily Report Sheet" and individual index card (see page 61).

Longer projects will obviously involve larger budgets and more complicated training programs, with opportunities to create a long-range, grass-roots voters' organization, follow-up work, evaluations, etc.

Participants in an educational campaign, especially if they live together (as in a single house), will want to set up a steering committee, hold regular evaluations of their work, discuss how they are getting along with local citizens (and with each other), and allow for some recreational and reading time. They should bring with them, among other things, a suit or (for girls) a dress suitable for attending a local church. Organizations sponsoring educational efforts should make every effort to inform participants in projects of the local voting and registration laws, deadlines, etc.

In canvassing for citizens to register to vote, or actually to vote, workers must remember that mothers with children to care for must have someone to watch the children while they are out of the house. One way of doing this is to have a "chain" in which the first mother to return home sits for the neighbor, who then returns to sit for her neighbor, etc. Car-pools to take groups of people while other workers act as baby-sitters are another method. Remember that the pulpit, the factory gate, the shopping center, and the street corner (especially during evenings) are natural locations to urge citizens to register to vote, if these locations are properly approached and properly used. Free films and leaflets should not be neglected—both are occasionally available from friendly trade unions. Churches may lend the use of mimeograph machines and typewriters.

Ultimately, the purpose of voter registration is to get people to vote, and to elect to various public offices candidates who

DAILY REPORT SHEET

List totals
1. Homes visited ....
2. Eligible voters (all over 21) ....
3. Nonregistered voters (eligible voters) ....
4. Registered voters ....

List totals and names
1. People to arrange transportation for ....
2. People volunteering transportation help ....
3. Families needing baby sitters ....
4. People volunteering baby sitting help ....

List comments, standard responses and problems,
direct quotes, sections of interviews.

INDIVIDUAL INDEX CARD

Address ....

Ward ....

Precinct ....

Phone ....

Date of visit(s) ....

Persons not registered

....

....

....

....

Persons who need to re-register

....

....

....

Plans to register or re-register

....

....

....

....

Services offered:

Services needed:

Not at home, revisit ....

Comment (need to talk further, unusual occupations, etc.) ....

....

Worker(s): ....

will accurately represent the interests of the electorate. Since resources are limited, you will not be involved in any and every voting district in which there may be low registration or participation in elections. Frequently candidates appealing to the Negro vote may not be to your liking, but because they represent at least a small step towards the political education of the community, or because they represent at least an alternative to a racist, you will be put in the position of having to support them. This does not mean you have to support everything they say or do—but remember that you are an outsider, and that your criticisms must make sense locally if you are not to isolate yourself from the very community which you seek to help educate.

Remember, too, that in many Southern states there are, percentage-wise, as many poor whites excluded from politics as Negroes. At one time, in the 1870's and 1880's, there was a powerful alliance in the South between poor whites and the ex-slave population. The final objective of current campaigns to refranchise the Negro and poor white is to resurrect that alliance, to forge a political force in the South which will be, by its nature, liberal, pro-trade union, pro-social services, pro-civil rights, and in the long run for a positive foreign policy and for peace. Because such a force will have to do away with the present Dixiecrat blockade of progressive legislation in Washington, it will have a profound and long-lasting influence on all of American life. Your part in voter registration, even though it may seem minute, helps to forge this political force.

6 / WORKSHOPS IN DIRECT ACTION

The workshop is different from a conference or an educational meeting in that its goal is to involve all of the participants in the practical application of skills, rather than lecturing *to* them or giving them pure theory. Workshops may involve lectures and theory as part of the schedule, but the real aim is practice. The kind of participation in a workshop may vary—from leaders attempting fully to draw out and involve members of an audience, to breaking up into work sessions or "buzz" groups, to "role-playing." Most workshops will involve all of these, plus some lecture or panel discussion sessions. The particular concern of this chapter is role-playing. Obviously, for best results it is necessary to keep the size of workshops down in order to involve all of the participants—yet workshops must be large enough to profit from a variety of personalities and talents.

There are five good reasons for workshops, and particularly for role-playing:

(1) *To practice skills.* Participants, by taking on various roles, learn how to behave in different situations. They get an idea of what to expect and how to react in the best way (to obtain best results). Mistakes are less likely later on. Going into the streets, into unfamiliar surroundings and new situations without some training and understanding of the principles involved is as foolish as going into a ball game without knowing the signals or the rules.

(2) *To understand your opponent.* By playing opponents' roles, the worker gets to feel how the opponent thinks and feels. This will be of tremendous value in the real situation, because the worker will be better able to make judgments as to possible reactions to various tactics. It is particularly important prior to conducting negotiations, because the negotiator will be prepared for some of the answers and arguments from the opposition. Tactics that deal more realistically with how the opponent actually thinks are more likely to develop this way.

(3) *To build up morale.* By practicing a variety of situations with the people who will be with you in action, you'll get to know each other better and build up confidence in what each member of the group is likely to do under pressure. In the face of tremendous hostility it is crucial to have confidence in the other members of your group. The group, as it works together to prepare for an action, builds up this confidence, or morale.

(4) *To get rid of tensions.* Everybody, particularly the victim of segregation, has tensions. It is important, when in action, to keep tensions under control. But in a crisis situation tensions tend to build up and come out. People "crack" under strain and "blow up." After a while, some begin to suffer the equivalent of "battle fatigue." Obviously this presents a real danger if it takes place in an actual situation. In the workshop the opportunity is created to get rid of tensions *before* the action. Everybody has a chance to blow off steam in a harmless place. Frequently this happens when participants "let go" at other partici-

pants who are playing the roles of opponents: police officers, members of the white power structure, "Uncle Toms," etc. (Joking and singing also help to do this.)

(5) *To make for more democracy*. The workshop, by spreading skills to a larger number, helps to build a larger body of persons who are familiar with the techniques and skills of leadership (running a meeting, conducting negotiations, being a picket captain, acting as a spokesman). Leadership is helped to move out from a single person to others, who, because of their know-how, will have to be brought into the decision-making process. If an organization lacks fuller participation only because there is little know-how, workshops can be deliberately set up to begin the process of making the group more democratic.

THE AUDIENCE AND THE SOCIO-DRAMA

Role-playing, or socio-drama (not to be confused with psycho-drama, which is used primarily as a technique for mental health), requires an audience as well as participants, but the audience must be cautioned not to laugh or react. They are the observers and will be asked to evaluate and comment after the "scenario" is concluded. The socio-drama involves two or more persons spontaneously acting out roles in the context of real problems which the group faces. It can be used by anybody, for just about any human relations situation. Role-playing also requires the presence of a leader or director.

It is the job of the leader to (a) define the problem; (b) establish the situation, or scene ("scenario"); (c) cast the characters; (d) brief and warm up the actors and observers; (e) commence the action; (f) cut the action when he thinks the point has been made; (g) lead the discussion and analysis of the situation and the behavior of the participants by getting them and the audience to talk; (h) make notes and plan future tests of the lessons learned from the scenario.

Being a leader is difficult, and good leadership requires experience. Beginning leaders should not be discouraged if a scenario fizzles. But note what went wrong, and learn from mistakes. There are a number of books now available on this technique (frequently used in industrial relations) and use should be made of them by those interested in specializing in this valuable leadership function.*

It is wise to begin with simple situations, perhaps not even directly related to immediate problems (e.g., an argument between two boys as to whether to rumble with the gang or go on the picket line), in order to "warm up" the group. Do not let the scenario go on too long—cut it off when you think the group has seen enough to be able to analyze the problem, or when there is a natural ending or when there is a dead end because of bad casting or inaccurate briefing or misunderstanding.

Also make sure that if you are doing a series of scenarios there is a good "mix" between talk and action. Have some scenarios which emphasize each. After the scenario is concluded, during stage (g), make sure you pin down what has been learned. Summarize for the group, then move on to the next scenario. Some scenarios are worth repeating with a different cast of characters, bringing in lessons learned just before.

An interesting, quick way to warm up an audience is "Phillips 66": the audience is broken into groups of six; each member of the group introduces himself (so you get acquainted); then the group appoints a spokesman. For six minutes the group makes quick comments or poses questions about a problem which the chairman of the meeting has assigned (What do you hope to get out of this workshop? What is the most urgent problem facing your group back home? Why are students apathetic to politics? Why nonviolence?). Then the spokesman from each group presents the comments or questions from the group to the whole audience. In this way the steering committee of the workshop or conference can quickly evaluate the quality and motivations of the participants, and can adjust the day's plans accordingly. The participants have been warmed up and introduced to each other at the same time.

* For example: Corsini, Shaw, and Blake, *Role-playing in Business and Industry,* Glencoe, Free Press, 1961; and the popularly written *Leadership and Dynamic Group Action,* by Beal, Bohlen, and Raudabaugh, Ames, Iowa State University Press, 1962.

It is important to get "feedback," not only in a workshop or conference but in any organization. Feedback means finding out how the group is getting along. This can be done by making use of an observer who records what goes on, by post-meeting questionnaires, through buzz-groups (like Phillips 66), or by interviews.

SAMPLE SCENARIOS FOR ROLE-PLAYING

1. The Eviction

A group of civil rights demonstrators is blocking access to a tenement to prevent a constable from evicting a tenant who has been participating in a rent strike. The constable and several citizens urge the group to obey the law and move out of the way; then the constable and a police officer threaten the group with arrest if it does not move. (You may want to continue this scenario to the point of actual arrest and being taken to the wagon.)

Questions: How do the demonstrators respond to the other citizens and to the constable? How do they respond to the officer?

Cast: Three or four demonstrators, two or three citizens, a constable, one or more police officers.

2. The Congressman

Congressman Blank, a Negro representing a predominantly Negro district—with a do-nothing record so far, and a reputation for being a "tool" of the local political machine—is having a change of heart. He has even gone so far as to invite a group of civil rights people to his office in order to get their ideas. He has a group of his own advisers present. The congressman, the civil rights people, and the congressman's advisers discuss the issue in a hard-headed, unsentimental way.

Questions: What will the relationship of the civil rights people be to the congressman and his staff? How will the congressman and his staff react to the ideas presented? What kind of information is needed in order to present a coherent case to the congressman?

Cast: Congressman, two staff persons, three or four civil rights persons.

3. The Barber Shop

A Negro civil rights demonstrator is attempting to integrate a barber shop. All other participants in the situation are whites: a barber, an assistant, two clients in the chairs, one client waiting, one police officer. All the whites are segregationists, but one of the whites in the chair is particularly rabid. The action begins when the *other* white is finished and gets up. It is the Negro's turn, but the head barber calls "you're next" to the waiting white client.

Questions: What is the response of the Negro client? What kinds of actions and remarks raise and lower tensions? How does the segregationist *really* see the situation? What does he really feel? What are the real issues as far as he is concerned? As far as the civil rights demonstrator is concerned?

Cast: As listed above. You may add an additional onlooker (white) who sympathizes with the Negro and who intervenes at a later point in the action in order to show how this will affect the situation.

4. Magistrate's Court

A group of civil rights demonstrators has been arrested for "disturbing the peace" and "refusing to obey an officer" in a demonstration involving a school boycott. The action was peaceful picketing, but some of the demonstrators came in without training, and in fact did call out, jeer, and step onto school property. The officers had ordered them off the property; they had refused to get off and had been arrested with some of the "regulars" on the picket line. The scene is magistrate's court the next morning. The action begins when the magistrate asks, "Who is the complaining officer in this case?"

Questions: What is the relationship of the regular demonstrators to the undisciplined demonstrators? How should the defense be handled (assume that one of the "regulars" is an attorney)? What should be the attitude of the group toward the officer? Toward the magistrate? In case of conviction, what should the group's policy be? You may want to divide the scenario in half—the court scene, and a discussion among the defendants as to policy.

Cast: Four "regular" demonstrators; two "undisciplined," newcomer demonstrators, a magistrate, a police officer, a court clerk or bailiff, several newsmen and other onlookers.

5. Sit-In

Six demonstrators, including one white boy and one white girl, sit at a lunch counter in a Southern community in an effort to secure service. A white waitress does not serve them. Two white troublemakers come and harass the demonstrators. A policeman stands by but does not interfere. There are some other people at the counter. The action begins when the demonstrators take their seats.

Questions: What is the effect of refusal of service upon the demonstrators? What is the effect of heavy harassment? How do the demonstrators see the situation? What of the effects on the onlookers?

Cast: Six demonstrators, white waitress, troublemakers, police officer, two or three other white customers.

6. The Cell

A white civil rights demonstrator has just been arrested in a Southern civil rights demonstration. Since the jail is segregated, he is lodged in a cell with three other white men, all of whom are ardent segregationists. The segregationists are sitting on the two bottom bunks, and one has his feet on the only chair in the place. Action begins when a police officer, with appropriate remarks, pushes the demonstrator into the cell.

Questions: How do you communicate your ideas in a hostile environment and still survive? What kinds of techniques might be developed to help in this situation?

Cast: Police officer, white demonstrator, three other white men.

7. Committee Meeting

A meeting of a local civil rights organization's emergency executive committee is taking place to discuss what appears to have been the murder of a Negro citizen while on his way to the police station in a police car. One member of the committee has been in touch with the local chapter of the American Civil Liberties Union and has an approximate idea of what happened, but the others have chiefly rumors. There is considerable community sentiment to take action. Another community civil rights group has already announced a march on city hall, and it is known that some of the marchers will be armed and that the march will be without any real discipline. One member of the committee is solidly in sympathy with this tactic already. The problem is to work out a tactic for the whole group.

Questions: What should the group do about the other civil rights group, if anything? What should be the group's attitude toward the potential for community violence? What kinds of tactics can the group effectively undertake?

Cast: Five persons, integrated. One of these is informed on what actually happened. Another has already made up his mind on what tactic to follow. One person is chairman.

8. The Picket Line

Any group up to about twenty-five may participate. The instructor picks an issue and a situation, and gives instructions for the group to walk an elongated circle, a few feet apart. It is helpful to have signs. Picket captains are assigned for each end of the line. An information officer is assigned, and a captain-in-charge is assigned. A variety of situations may be explored:

(1) harassment by segregationists, including roughing up, taking signs away, name-calling
(2) questions from passers-by
(3) volunteeer unknown to the group arrives to join the line
(4) drunk passes the group and makes remarks
(5) persons from other integrationist groups not committed to nonviolence arrive with their signs
(6) harassment from police officers, including ordering the group across the street in violation of civil liberties
(7) newspapermen attempt to question pickets
(8) single picket becomes ill, or becomes violent (instructor may "plant" a person in the group)

Questions: How are decisions made on-the-spot? How are decisions communicated to the group? How are public relations maintained?

9. The March

This is a situation involving only four persons and demonstrating the problem of decision-making on-the-spot. One of the participants is told he is in charge of a mass march on city hall; at a mass meeting the night before it was democratically decided, for various reasons, not to have signs of any kind in the march. The march is about to "take off" when three persons appear, in succession, with signs. They are not connected with each other. The first person is privately instructed to be very stubborn and non-cooperative about putting his sign away; the second is cooperative; the third is neutral. The first two were at the meeting the night before; the third was not. Action begins when the first person approaches the march marshal, and the marshal says, "Last night we agreed on no signs, right?" (He poses the same question to each of the others.) The instructor stops the action after the marshal has somehow come to grips with the stubborn individual, then the next person appears. In the course of the discussion with the third individual, the instructor calls out, "They're ready to go," referring to the march. It is important that the marshal not know in advance what the reaction of the three persons will be.

Questions: How do the marshal's feelings about the situation change as the pressure builds up? How much should the marshal try to placate the individuals, and how firm should he be? How does time affect the situation?

Cast: Marshal, three persons with signs.

10. The Riot

There is a race riot going on. Two Negro rioters have cornered a white person who was passing by and are taunting him (or her), intending then to assault him (or her) physically. A third Negro comes upon the scene and attempts to persuade the rioters to "lay off."

Variations: Make the person coming on the scene white; reverse the riot to make the two rioters white and the victim Negro, with the person coming on the scene first white, then Negro.

Questions: How does the victim feel? What can the person coming on the scene say or do? How does changing his race affect the situation? Why are the rioters rioting? Why do they feel as intensely as they do? (This goes whether the rioters are Negro or white.)

Cast: Two rioters, victim, person coming on the scene (varying racially).

7 / DIRECT ACTION TACTICS

One catalog of nonviolent action lists some sixty-four different methods which have been used throughout history.* We are taking from this list those which seem most significant for the current civil rights struggle.

DEMONSTRATIONS

Demonstrations are primarily expressions of a point of view, and do not of themselves change the power structure as vigorously as non-cooperation or direct intervention might. Nevertheless, they do go beyond verbal protest and are considered sufficiently threatening by many authorities to provoke harsh reprisals.

1. Marches and parades

Technically, the difference between a march and a parade is that a march has a destination of symbolic or immediate importance to the cause, whereas a parade route is chosen for convenience or potential impact on a neighborhood. Both may be short or long. Mass marches and parades can express the solidarity of the campaigners and be an important morale-booster.

A common way of discrediting marches and parades is to describe them as disorderly and violent. You can take two steps to eliminate the validity of this charge:

(a) Have either silence, or singing in unison. Both make a powerful impression of unity and dignity. Slogan-shouting and conversation build an impression of disunity and disorder.

(b) Set up a system of leadership. Experience shows it is helpful to have a marshal and a number of line leaders who, once

* Gene Sharp, *Methods of Nonviolent Action,* Institute for Social Research, Oslo, Norway.

policy is set, follow the directions of the marshal. The leadership helps in two ways: keeping discipline and building the morale of the marchers. In addition, more efficient decisions can be made in the event of police interference, etc. Leaders should be clearly designated and should set an example for others to follow.

A long march is often called a walk. The best known civil rights walk is the one postman William Moore began through the South, which others continued when he was killed. The Committee for Nonviolent Action has organized two walks for peace and freedom through the South which had to contend with cattle-prods and the like. The effect of a walk can be somewhat like that of the Freedom Rides—to dramatize an issue and give a morale boost to the movement in the towns through which the walkers go.

2. Picketing and Vigiling

The difference between picketing and a vigil is that a vigil is longer and held in a meditative spirit. Often a vigil is held around-the-clock for several days, or it may be daily for weeks or even months. It is also customary for participants in a vigil to stand rather than walk, as in picketing. In a culture like ours where religion is held in high esteem, a vigil is sometimes more effective than picketing; however, it is slightly more wearying and requires more self- and group-discipline. The remarks about orderliness apply here, to both picketing and vigiling.

SAMPLE PICKET OR VIGIL DISCIPLINE *

We will try to maintain an attitude of good will at all times, especially in face of provocation.

If violence occurs against us, we will not retaliate but will try to practice forgiveness and forbearance.

We agree that one person is in charge of specific actions and agree to abide by the decisions of the person in charge, even if at the time we do not fully agree with or understand the decision.

If in good conscience we cannot comply with this decision, we will not take contrary action but will withdraw from that phase.

* Slightly revised from Charles C. Walker, *Organizing for Nonviolent Direct Action.*

In the event of arrest, we will submit with promptness and composure.

We will try to be prompt in our appointments and to carry out responsibly the tasks we have been assigned.

Here are some suggestions which will help you to organize an effective picket line.*

(1) Assemble somewhere other than the place where the picket line will be, then go to the place in a group; this avoids confusion and gives the leader a chance to pass out printed copies of the discipline (see sample discipline in this chapter) as well as to conduct registration.

(2) Ask participants to refer questioners, press, or police to the marshal or information officer.

(3) Expect participants to walk erectly and not slouch, call out, laugh loudly, or use profanity; smoking may be ruled out in some situations.

(4) Assign two leafleteers to each location, so leafleting can go on if one leafleteer gets involved with a questioner.

(5) Instruct leafleteers on how to answer very briefly when asked "What is this all about?" or "Who's doing this?" or "Why don't you people go back to Russia?" or other questions.

(6) Ask leafleteers to pick up all discarded leaflets (to avoid legal entanglements and to show good will).

(7) Keep leaflets in a plastic bag in rainy weather.

(8) Avoid unnecessary scurrying about.

(9) Give instructions in a clear and authoritative voice, but avoid a domineering approach.

(10) Remember that your conduct sets an example for others.

3. Fraternization

This technique has been used in countries occupied by a foreign power, as well as in this country. The idea is to go out of the way to talk with the police or other opponents in a friendly way and to try to persuade them that one's cause is just. Where it has been tried it has on occasion been amazingly

* This listing is based on Charles Walker's *Organizing for Nonviolent Direct Action.*

AN ORGANIZED PICKET LINE

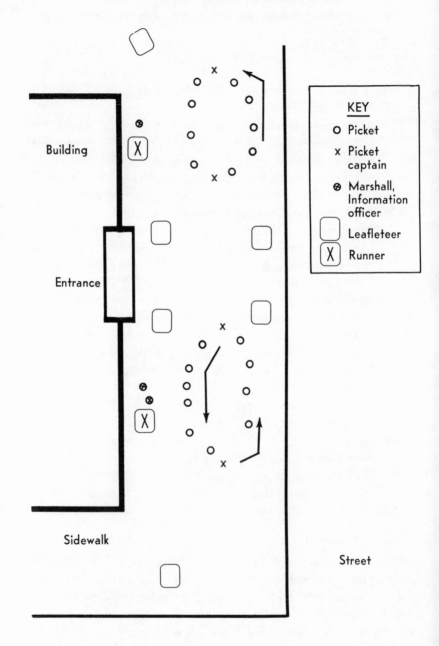

effective, as some instances in Norway under the Nazi occupation testify. But it is not easy.

In the summer of 1964 a group of pacifists conducted a direct action project at a missile site in Quebec Province, Canada, including vigiling and civil disobedience. One of the techniques which they used to communicate was to pass out leaflets addressed "to our brothers in the armed forces," and "to our brothers in the police force." They also made impromptu speeches when soldiers and police were near, explaining their motivation and purpose. As a result, there was some breakdown in military discipline as soldiers went out of their way to join the pacifists in a prayer meeting at the conclusion of the vigil.

4. "Haunting"

This is a means of reminding officials of the immorality of their behavior—volunteers follow them everywhere they go. In India during the Gandhian struggles arrests were made, but the volunteers were replaced by others who "haunted" the authorities until officials were sick of it.

5. Leafleting

Leafleting can do several things for the cause: (a) provide the people with more accurate information than they get in the newspapers; (b) give more people more personal contact with the campaigners (in large communities many people never actually see demonstrators); (c) involve children and others who otherwise might not actively participate in the struggle.

6. Renouncing honors

There can be some symbolic impact when campaigners renounce honors given them in the past. For example, Negro veterans might send back medals of honor; a Negro "Woman of the Year" might refuse the award from an institution which is part of the power structure; Negro students might send back their American Legion School Awards.

Some of the techniques which come under the heading of demonstrations may become civil disobedience if the city declares them illegal. Injunctions may be issued by courts forbidding marches or picketing. Where the Constitution is in operation, however, these methods do not usually involve breaking the law.

NON-COOPERATION

This general category involves methods of direct action in which the campaigners withdraw their usual degree of cooperation with the opponent. The methods may be legal or illegal, depending on local laws.

1. Strike

The strike is one of the best known of all forms of direct action. It has not, however, been used very often in the civil rights struggle. It would be most potent in those areas where Negroes form a very large part of the population or of some economic concern which is important to the area. A form of the strike which might be experimented with is the "token strike." In a token strike all those sympathetic to the cause go off the job for a brief time—perhaps one day or a few hours. This is a way of showing solidarity and seriousness of purpose.

2. Hartal

The Indians under Gandhi developed this device extensively, but it was also used in Budapest at the beginning of the 1956 Hungarian revolution. A Hartal involves staying at home for a full day or more, leaving factories, streets, and places of amusement totally empty. In addition to reducing the chances of "incidents," the stay-at-home may serve to demonstrate to the opponent the degree of unity and self-discipline among the people. In a campaign which stresses religious aspects, the day can be seen as a time for meditation and purification.

3. Consumers' Boycott or Selective Buying

From the Montgomery Bus Boycott on, the consumers' boycott has played an important role in the civil rights struggle. This method has its roots in the American Revolution and even further back in history, and has been used throughout the world.

Its effectiveness depends on how much the businessman needs the campaigners' patronage for his economic survival.

Here are the advantages of the boycott: (a) it minimizes violence; (b) it promotes solidarity; (c) it does not usually involve civil disobedience. On the other hand, it usually requires a good deal of unity on the part of the protesting community.

4. Renters' Boycott (Rent-Strike)

The refusal to pay rent because of grievances against a landlord may be for a short period (token boycott) or indefinitely. Irish peasants in 1879 were often evicted for refusing rents to rich English landlords. Whether or not eviction takes place depends partly on the number of persons participating and on the nature of the local laws.

In the current civil rights struggle, workers go from house to house, apartment to apartment, talking with people about the injustice of their situation. They invite tenants to an area or house meeting, where the possibilities of united action are stressed. Those who will commit themselves at the meeting begin to strike at once—there is little to be gained by setting a date in the future for the beginning of the action. The action of the few who first volunteer will hopefully begin a wave of others joining the strike.

Guidelines for organization include: being realistic in explaining to the tenants what may happen (no one can guarantee major repairs); staying in close contact with the tenants to offset intimidation; and planning to put the rent money "in escrow," or into a special fund set aside for this purpose. The fund should be carefully accounted for.

Local regulations differ as to eviction possibilities. It is important to get legal counsel, for often constables themselves break the law in the process of eviction. In addition to countering eviction by legal action, picketing the constable and living on the sidewalk in front of the house are direct action tactics which may be tried; numbers of tenants can also obstruct constables' access to the house, thus preventing eviction. This is generally against the law, of course.

5. School boycott

One of the advantages of the school boycott is that it involves the children in a struggle which will result in their eventual benefit, while still not involving them in a front-line confrontation with its accompanying dangers. The setting up of freedom schools for teaching the young can be a valuable exercise for those in the Negro community who are otherwise difficult to involve.

6. Tax refusal

This is a drastic tactic, yet it has often been used in struggles in the past in various parts of the world. It can be partial, such as withholding school taxes, or complete. The money which would otherwise go for taxes can be given to the movement for distribution to needy campaigners. Generally opponents feel this tactic more deeply than almost any other, for if the refusing population is large it threatens the very survival of the government. Harsh reprisal may therefore be expected. Despite this, the strong moral appeal involved ("Why pay the police who are beating you?") and the strength of the tactic has made tax refusal effective in some campaigns.

INTERVENTION

Direct nonviolent intervention consists of physical confrontation rather than withdrawal of cooperation or demonstrating. It carries the conflict into the opponent's camp and often changes the status quo abruptly.

1. Sit-in

The sit-in has been used in the U.S. mostly in restaurants and at lunch counters. Generally campaigners progressively occupy a large number of all of the available seats and refuse to leave until the Negro members of the group are served, the restaurant closes, the group is arrested, or a certain fixed period of time has gone by. This method can also be used in other situations such as on buses and trains, as in the Freedom Rides. There have been

DIRECT ACTION TACTICS   81

sit-ins in the offices of notables such as mayors and business executives in order to obtain appointments or to symbolize the blocking of freedom in which the official is participating. Legislative halls can be used similarly. Often the sit-in is a perfectly legal activity.

NONVIOLENT DISCIPLINE OF THE 1960 NASHVILLE
STUDENT SIT-IN MOVEMENT

Don't strike back or curse if abused.
Don't laugh out.
Don't hold conversations with floor workers.
Don't leave your seats until your leader has given you instruction to do so.
Don't block entrances to the stores and the aisles.
Show yourself courteous and friendly at all times.
Sit straight and always face the counter.
Report all serious incidents to your leader.
Refer all information to your leader in a polite manner.
Remember love and nonviolence.
May God bless each of you.

Allied methods are the stand-in, where people line up for admission to a theater or similar place; the wade-in, in which campaigners attempt to swim at a segregated beach; and the kneel-in, in which Negroes try to worship at a church which excludes them.

2. The fast

The fast was used as a method of psychological intervention by, among others, Danilo Dolci* when he led 1,000 unemployed fishermen in a twenty-four-hour mass fast on a beach in Sicily. The fast can be of heightened effectiveness when undertaken by persons of high status, such as ministers. Gandhi, the best-known faster, considered this the most difficult of all techniques and emphasized that it should be thought through carefully. This is especially true of the fast unto death. Experience with the fast in Albany, Georgia, by peace walkers, indicates

*Dolci, sometimes called "the Italian Gandhi," is a pioneer in applying direct action to community organization.

that clarity of purpose and realistic time periods are important. Efforts must be made to overcome the misunderstanding which comes in a society where "good living" is prized and self-denial is looked down upon.

Gandhi believed that fasting is most effective when there is a close relationship between the faster and the opponent.

3. Reverse strike

This method has been found effective in various situations— e.g., agricultural workers have done more work and worked longer hours than they were paid for, in support of their demand for pay increases. The unemployed in Sicily in 1956 voluntarily repaired a public road that was badly in need of repair in order to call attention to the severe unemployment in the area and the government's failure to deal with it. Although this method looks harmless enough at first glance, it has in practice been regarded as a sufficient threat so that reverse-strikers have been arrested, imprisoned, and even in some cases shot by police attempting to stop them from working! Clearing an unused lot for a playground, despite the fact that the lot belongs to someone else, or to the city, might be a current example. This may involve breaking the law.

4. Nonviolent interjection and obstruction

This involves placing one's body between another person and the objective of his work. Civil rights workers in this country have used it at school and other construction sites, to protest the building itself or discrimination in hiring the construction workers. Striking hosiery workers in Reading, Pennsylvania, in 1957, lay down on the sidewalks at the factory gates making it necessary for non-strikers to walk over them to get into the factory, or else stay away from their jobs. In early 1964 at a Cleveland construction site several actionists lay down in front of a bulldozer; a minister, Rev. Bruce Klunder, seeing that the operator might reverse direction, lay down behind the bulldozer and was killed. We should remember that in a confusing situation the operator might not look in both directions before moving his machine.

There is more danger of injury or death when one or a few persons engage in interjection than when a great many participate. An example of the latter case, called obstruction, occurred in Japan in 1956 when 10,000 people physically occupied a site intended for a U.S. air base. After several days of obstruction the plans for building the air base were abandoned.

Even while this manual is being prepared some individual or group is probably devising still other forms of nonviolent direct action. One of the elements of non-violence is the creativity which it stimulates, and the reader will probably want to experiment with new forms of nonviolent struggle. Not all of them will be really effective, and some will collapse as did the World's Fair "stall-in" in April, 1964. In evaluating a new tactic before trying it out, the thoughtful civil rights worker will ask:

(1) Is it clearly related to the issue?
(2) Are the people it will inconvenience really the people heavily involved in the injustice?
(3) Is there chance of direct confrontation between the campaigners and the opponent?
(4) Does the tactic put a major part of the suffering which is inevitable in social change upon our shoulders, rather than upon innocent bystanders?
(5) If direct action, especially interjection and obstruction, involve violation of the law (civil disobedience), are demonstrators prepared to accept the penalties in order to make the point?

If the answer to these questions is "yes," the tactic may be worth trying.

8 / COUNTER-DEMONSTRATION OPERATIONS

The authors have had only limited experience with some of the more serious types of counter-demonstration operations (police and mob violence against public demonstrations), so it would be foolish of us to give a lot of "advice." A number of experts have suggested that in any case one should not become too preoccupied with trying to cope with police tactics, because such efforts keep you from the basic objectives of nonviolent demonstrations. They bog you down in trying to outguess the police, and you lose sight of the basic goals—to promote a society of justice. There are, however, some ideas which can increase the effectiveness of civil rights workers when faced with police and mob violence, or at least cut the physical risks, while maintaining the basic integrity of the demonstration and its participants.*

Remember that the opponent would like, if possible, to provoke your group into wild statements, inaccurate or exaggerated accusations which cannot be proved, name-calling, confusion, undignified and disorderly behavior, in-fighting among the leaders, desertion from the ranks, and outright violent retaliation. In trying to avoid being provoked into these actions, some elementary rules will help:

(1) Improve the educational and organizational tools by which violence can be contained and prevented. These include workshops and other training, discipline, and loyalty to the group and what it stands for.

* The following points are again based on Charles Walker's *Organizing for Nonviolent Direct Action.*

(2) In a demonstration, remember to act only upon instructions from assigned leaders. Do not break ranks except to help an injured person.

(3) If you are the victim of an attack, and are not too severely disabled, you can still take nonviolent initiatives. For instance, in a calm voice you might say, "Sir, may I ask you a question?" If someone else is being attacked, you might go to the attacker and divert him from his victim in a similar way.

(4) Remember that you must be more than calm and restrained. You must also be creative and look for new ways to take nonviolent initiatives in the spirit of the goals and ideals of the movement. A group might, for instance, spontaneously begin singing a hymn together if an attack occurs.

(5) It is the authors' opinion that demonstrators should not appeal to the police for help at the scene of a demonstration. If police do not of their own accord protect the civil liberties of demonstrators, they likely will not help anyway. They may intervene only to stop the demonstration—and that should be your decision, not theirs. If we are to build a society of justice and brotherhood, we must learn to do our own "policing" and not depend upon the police of the local power structure.

STRATEGY AND THE POLICE

Police policy varies rather widely from state to state, from city to city, and even within cities from time to time. It varies from states in which conferences of police officials hear representatives of civil rights and peace groups explain their policies, to states where there is no communication, much less understanding, between demonstrators and police officials.

By police we include here police operations engaged in by units of the State and National Guard. Federal troops have been used in only a few cases, notably Little Rock and the University of Mississippi. Civil right workers will want to remember that in the latter case Negro troops were systematically

excluded from duty at the University, resulting in considerable unrest and, according to a confidential informant, a near mutiny at one point. As individuals, federal troops generally will tend to be friendly to the civil rights movement partly because of the nature of their duty, partly because of their racial composition, and partly because they resent local hostility which is aimed at them by segregationists. On the other hand, there is little reason to hope that the simple presence of federal troops will necessarily change the local situation; more likely the situation will only be "frozen" at its present point, and all demonstrations (including those by civil rights groups) banned. Local resentment of federal "occupation" may in fact be turned against local movements once federal protection is removed.

Bad policing can involve either the lack of police protection, resulting in the formation of mobs (as in the case of the Freedom Riders in Alabama in 1961), or in the use of the police themselves to crush civil rights demonstrations while at the same time forbidding vigilante action by mobs. The latter system has the advantage of being not only more efficient, but also proceeding under the protection of "law and order." While Northern police rarely use the former system it should not be thought that they never use the latter. There are at least two variations upon this system—the straightforward, "hard" line:

disperse, or else. Period. The other variation appears soft on the surface and attempts to disarm, psychologically, the leadership and rank-and-file by being polite first, and only later pulling off the soft gloves. For example, the police command may appear to side with the demonstrators, asking them to sing a few songs or lead the group in prayer (this was the tactic of the Maryland State Guard in Cambridge in May, 1964), before asking them politely to disperse. This can be coupled with veiled threats to have leading demonstrators committed for observation to mental institutions, which happened in Cambridge and also during the Harlem riots in July, 1964—this threat seems to be more severe than simple prison. But the objective is the same: to disperse demonstrators at all costs.

Given the basic objective of the civil rights movement in a demonstration—namely to publicize a wrong, confront the community with the facts, and sometimes create dislocation in order to secure action—police tactics are only half of the picture. The leadership ability, perspectives, and organization of the civil rights demonstrators are also important. The best possible combination is to have a well-organized, well-educated movement, combined with generally accepted and legal police tactics. The worst is to have neither. Most demonstrations fall somewhere in between. But even under the worst kind of police reprisal, if the movement is well disciplined the basic objective need not be lost. Basic objectives can be lost in a host of charges and counter-charges if the movement is disorganized, no matter how enlightened the police may be.

Discipline which maximizes the basic objectives of a demonstration involves a well-organized demonstration with clear lines of command and communication, and with a clear understanding by the participants of what they are to do in a variety of circumstances. Communicating, or at least trying to communicate, the objectives of the demonstration not only to the general public but also to the police command in advance is considered an important part of organization. A dignified bearing at all times is also important, particularly when making physical contact with police units. Calling a demonstration off at a particular point, or retreating in the face of police or mob violence is perfectly okay; but it should be done by prearranged plan, and in as orderly a manner as possible under the circumstances. This points up the "image" of the movement and makes it more difficult to charge the civil rights group with being nothing but a "rabble" commanded by "irresponsible agitators." Dignity also has a very definite effect upon police and onlookers, and tends to break down their prejudiced notions about the movement. Nonviolent tactics are an essential part of a dignified demonstration, and even of an orderly retreat.

POLICE TACTICS

Here are some comments on "Counter-Demonstration Operations" in terms of specific tactics used by police, so that you will have some idea of the kinds of things you may expect.

Police and troops, once they have been given their orders, do not care about the objective of a demonstration. They look only at the behavior of the demonstrators: Is this a crowd, a mob, or a riot? A crowd is just a large group of people; a crowd in motion, usually because of a leader, an incident, the appearance of a hated individual or a symbol, is a mob. A riot is a disturbance by three or more persons who want to overcome opposition to their action by lawful or unlawful means.

Accepted American police practices involve a plan to cope with demonstrations, acting with all the force necessary to carry out the plan. Intelligent offiers do not use more force than necessary, as it only angers individuals and crowds, and they do not bluff. They know that it is smarter to arrest random citizens off the edge of a crowd, rather than try to move into the center to arrest, say, a street speaker. (But in a New York anti-Civil Defense demonstration this did not work; demonstrators proceeded to offer themselves for arrest in large numbers.) Officers who follow accepted practices make their intentions clear to the crowd or demonstration, allow time to clear out, and leave avenues of escape (unlike a recent Peruvian sports stadium tragedy in which gas panicked a crowd against barred doors).

Authorities on riot control advocate the following course of action: a show of force (assembling large numbers of police), an order to disperse, use of nightsticks, use of tear gas and/or fire hoses and/or horses, and, as a last resort, the use of fire-arms. Authorities, both police and army, have said that live ammunition should not be fired over the heads of demonstrators or rioters—that is bluff, and it undermines the crowd's respect for police. (But New York police, during the Harlem riots of July, 1964, in fact ignored accepted practices, used neither gas nor fire hoses nor horses, and opened fire over the heads of rioters on a large scale.)

A crowd is usually attacked opposite the direction in which police want to drive it. A skirmish line, wedge, or diagonal line is formed across the street, and state, National Guard, and federal troops usually fix bayonets. The effort will be to drive the crowd or demonstration away from sensitive areas, street crossings, and objectives of demonstrations such as stores, and to break the crowd into its individual units by the use of gas, horses, dogs, fire hoses, etc. Individuals can be more easily controlled and sent home than larger groups.

A demonstration is attacked by police or by a mob; a mob is *itself* doing the attacking, and is therefore a different matter. While it is difficult to disperse a mob, it should not be thought that civil rights workers can have no effect on a mob. Persons with loud voices can divert a mob from one target to another—and this can be done either for good or bad purposes. A well-coordinated team, communicating by means of walkie-talkies, can succeed in moving a mob around obstacles such as police barricades—again either for good or bad purposes. But it is almost impossible to urge a crowd to go home before it is "ready" to disperse. Crowds which verge on being mobs, and mobs themselves, do not like to listen to the voice of moderation. This is why Louis Napoleon built wide boulevards in Paris—so that cannon could have good aim at street demonstrators and mobs.

The Indian Shanti Sena (Peace Army) is, however, experimenting with nonviolent methods of mob dispersal. In Ahmedabad, for example, a group of Shanti Sainiks formed a wedge

A STANDARD POLICE RIOT PLAN

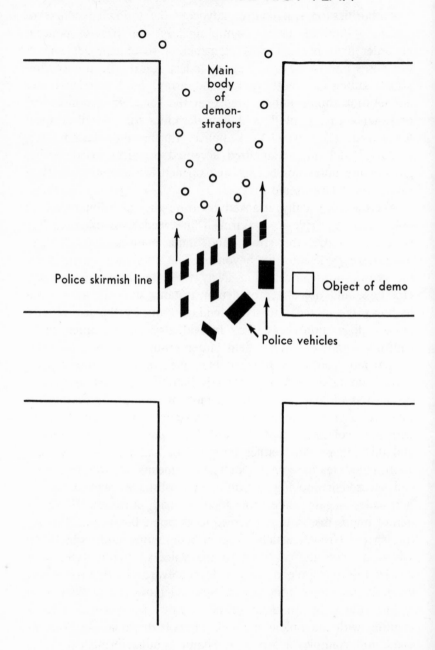

and went between the Hindu and Moslem mobs who were fighting. They were beaten by both sides initially, but the mobs soon realized that the Shanti Sainiks were not the "right people" to be beating, and stopped in confusion. This tactic allows an opportunity for speaking out and leading the mob into some other form of activity, such as a demonstration, or into dispersal.

Tear gas: Chloracetophenone (CN), or a more powerful version, CS, or Diphenylamine (DM or Adamsite), are termed "harassing agents" and are usually used in grenade form to demoralize, panic, and disperse crowds, mobs, and demonstrations. The effects of these gases extend beyond their visible cloud, and include a *severe* burning sensation in the eyes, choking, sneezing, headaches, and sometimes vomiting. There is no defense against gas attack except masks or leaving the area. The chief immediate reaction is to panic and run. This should be avoided at all costs. It may help you to know that harassing gases cannot cause permanent injury or death by themselves. Grasp the hands of demonstrators near you, and avoid running into the street (and risking getting run over since your visibility is impaired). Retreat in an orderly fashion from the scene. An assembly area should be picked beforehand and demonstrators should reassemble for further orders out of range of the gas. Clothing permeated with fumes should be changed. Persons affected by gas attack should face into the wind (assuming there is no further gas) and/or wash eyes and face in water (stick your head in a bucketful, if possible).

Horses, dogs: The chief purpose of using cavalry and dogs is also psychological, even though it may not seem that way to you. Some dogs are trained only to hold, not to bite, but don't count on it. If you are being held it is wise not to pull back sharply, as this may result in severe lacerations and further attack. There are a number of methods which have been used against dogs and horses, but the violence involved is such that we don't recommend trying them. As in the case of gas, the best system is to hold out as long as you can and retreat in an orderly way, and in as dignified a manner as possible under the circumstances. The same thing is true when cattle prods are used. This can be extremely painful, and you should not feel it is disgraceful to retreat. Let your opponents make contact with you, hold out as long as you think wise or possible, and retreat in an orderly fashion. Do not sit or lie down in front of horses unless you are prepared for severe, crippling injuries.

Fire hoses: This is similar, except that if you hold on in a human chain you may be able to withstand the pressure and not have to leave. Hosing is usually followed by other counter-demonstration operations, however.

SPECIAL PROBLEMS

Photographers: Police frequently try to intimidate or harass demonstrators by photographing them. In our opinion there can be no legitimate reason for this since demonstrating as such is legal under the Constitution. You will recognize police (or FBI) photographers because they take photographs of individual demonstrators rather than of the entire action. Regular newsmen are not interested in individuals and will generally be glad to identify themselves with press cards or union cards. In the long run there is not much point in evading having your picture taken (by keeping signs in front of your face, etc.), and you should not let the demonstration degenerate into a contest between you and the police photographer. On the other hand, you should not pose for group pictures to be taken by unidentified photographers. As for individual pictures, you will have to make a decision: shall evasive action be taken as a way of making a protest against an invasion of privacy? Or will you demonstrate the fact that you cannot be intimidated by openly, and with good will, permitting the police to "mug" you? This is a policy decision which you should discuss prior to a demonstration.

White participants: The white participant is singled out for special treatment by local opponents of the civil rights movement. As a white he is seen as a traitor, which is worse than being a Negro. His presence in the struggle serves to undermine the delicate structure of thinking and excuses which most white Southerners have created for themselves to account for segregation and discrimination. His presence by itself tells them their system is a lie. It is a shock. Therefore, it infuriates. It has to be accounted for: the white participant is seen as an outside agitator, a Communist, perhaps a light-skinned Negro, and, if a woman, a prostitute. For no real white person (read: no one from "our way of life") could walk with a sign, could "want a Negro to marry his sister." Violence, if it erupts, tends therefore to focus on the white picket. In prison, white inmates will tend to gang up on, and will sometimes try to beat up, white integrationist prisoners.

Meeting physical attack: There are two nonviolent reactions to a physical attack. One is to stand up to it and try to make eye contact with the attackers; the other is to fall down and cover up.

A leading practitioner of the first was John Wesley, founder of Methodism, who was frequently attacked by angry mobs in England. Wesley first threw off his hat so the mob could see his face. Next he developed eye contact with the mob generally. Then he'd find the leaders of the mob (usually in the front) and ask them questions like "What have I done to you?" "Do you know me?"* It is important in this first approach not to show fear, even though you will certainly feel it intensely. Wesley found this technique quite effective in avoiding serious beatings, and was often able to take the initiative and turn the incident into a victory for his cause.

The second approach is widely used. It is intended to protect the most vital parts of the body, through adopting a crouching position with hands over the head and ears, while lying on the ground. If a buddy is undergoing severe attack, and is on the ground, it is often wise to place yourself between the attackers and the victim by means of falling over the victim, face down, approximating the position of a person doing a "push-up" on the "up" part, but keeping your face down and tucked into your chest.

* Related by James Lawson, leader of the Nashville sit-ins.

RACE RIOTS, AND WHAT TO DO ABOUT THEM

There are three basic types of race riots in this country: (1) whites moving into Negro areas in order physically to harm individuals and property because they fear a Negro upsurge and seek to punish the Negro community for "getting out of line" (this is the basic Southern race riot, or "pogrom" pattern); (2) an interracial riot in which members of different groups meet on their borders, more or less on an equal basis, because they seek to protect or extend their "turf"; and (3) Negroes rioting within their own community, physically attacking whites in the area and white-owned and operated business establishments (including looting). The third was the pattern of the July, 1964, Harlem riot. Riots generally come to a halt as a result of tremendous police action to suppress it, sheer exhaustion of the rioters, or weather factors. The only effective way to *prevent* a riot is by eliminating the frustrations and deprivations which form the fertile soil for the specific incidents (sometimes manufactured by political groups with axes to grind) that set them off.

What can the civil rights worker, who is basically trying to eliminate the causes of riots, do once one has broken out? He should get into the area as soon as possible, since the police generally try to seal it off at an early stage. He should consider his own color in deciding his role. It is valuable to get someone of status among the authorities to work alongside him, for several reasons: the authorities will be getting a lot of telephone calls, including wild ones, and may take seriously only those from known persons. When a curfew is announced or a deserted-street order is passed, the civil rights worker will need to get an exemption. Also, the high-status person may help to get community demands for a hearing before the authorities.

If the worker knows the community he can organize a "Citizens Committee" to help coordinate constructive activity during the riot and channel grievances. Meeting a riot requires submerging organizational differences, so it is best not to link such a committee to an already existing organization. It should meet daily and report what is happening, sort out truth from rumor, and plan further action. It is sometimes wise to organize a demonstration to focus the attention of the city on the problem causing the riot, and to channel the activity of the people. A disciplined march to City Hall, for example, can use the energies of those otherwise involved in violence and looting.

A mass rally can be tried, at which the audience is organized by street blocks involving people signing up for specific jobs. This is helpful because people hesitate to participate in rioting once they lose their anonymity.

If the worker knows the gangs he should try to get to them and persuade them to stay off the streets and stop passing rumors. In the Philadelphia riots of 1964 the police picked up gang leaders; this can make the task of neutralizing the gangs more difficult.

If the worker does not know the community well enough to organize a community or work with the gangs, he can still *talk*—talk to everyone he sees, challenging rumors, urging people to get off the street and keep the children off. The worker's presence, talking to people and watching them, with a calm face, will be an influence. At one point in the Philadelphia riot a person was saved from youths because they were being watched so conspicuously as they waited for him to pass them.

There are three major problems the worker must face:

(1) *Rumors.* Riots often begin with rumors. The worker should challenge them and get to the rumor-mongers, if possible. Stick with the rumor-monger as he moves on to other opportunities.

Persuade people to go house-to-house contradicting rumors. Ministers, social workers, block leaders, housewives—anyone can help. The Citizens Committee will be the focus of this organizational work as it continues. If it is a large area, the house-to-house work will need to be supplemented by flyers and a telephone brigade.

The rumors are very often about police brutality. If the police are restrained in dealing with the riot the rumor can be challenged more easily than if the police use guns and in other ways shows that the rumor might have been true.

(2) *Looting.* This is very difficult to stem, but the presence on the street of respected community leaders may help to restrain it.

(3) *Violence.* Workers can organize a group to go about, rescuing persons being beaten. Usually, people who are using violence assume they have at least the silent support of the crowd which gathers. If the rescuers stand at several points in the crowd and loudly protest the beating, the mood can be changed and the violent persons confused and distracted. Then if the workers step in, they can carry the injured person away while the situation is still confused.

If the riot focuses on a certain location—for example, when a white mob gathers outside a house where Negroes have just moved in—high-status persons can place themselves between the mob and the house with real effectiveness. In Folcroft, Pennsylvania, in 1963, ministers stood in a vigil line in front of such a house despite the outcries of the enraged mob.

Another tactic in reducing violence is using group pressures where possible. For example, get block leaders to organize block peace committees who are determined to see that violence will not occur on *their* block.

Remember to put whites who are in danger into the homes of friendly Negroes, and vice versa. When members of one racial group are rioting, civil rights workers of a different color should generally be used chiefly in jobs on the sidelines, such as first aid, communications, and transportation.

Despite these suggestions, we should remember that riots are difficult to control, and the reader of this *Manual* may not have access to the large number of workers required really to dampen the riot completely. Still, it is better to have something positive to do in such situations than to do nothing or simply to stand on a soap box and suggest that the rioters go home. The non-violent organization, by acting in a hesitant or merely negative way (opposing "militancy") can sacrifice everything it has been working for by letting itself be discredited as an "Uncle Tom" group. It is important to try to work out positive and militant alternatives to a riot in advance. Surely we often have a good idea of the likelihood of a riot if we have any real contact with the community, and can prepare for it to some degree.*

SOME NOTES ON SECURITY IN THE DEEP SOUTH †

Travel

When persons leave their project, they should call the home project person-to-person on arrival at their destination *in person*. If they are reported missing, personnel should notify central headquarters. A system of daily reports should note all changes in personnel, transfers, etc. Phones should be used only when there is no time to use mail. Care should be taken to avoid using full names of persons over the phone. Checklists to keep track of all personnel at all times should be maintained. Use the "buddy" system so someone always knows where you are.

Doors of cars should be locked at all times. At night, windows should be rolled up as much as possible. Gas tanks should have locks and be kept locked. Hoods should also be locked.

No one should go *anywhere* alone, especially not in an automobile, or at night. Travel at night should be avoided unless absolutely necessary.

Remove all objects from your car which could be construed as weapons: hammers, files, iron rules, etc. No liquor bottles, beer cans, etc., should be inside your car. Do not travel with names and addresses of local contacts.

Know all roads in and out of town. Study the county map. Know locations of safe homes and contacts in the county.

When getting out of a car at night, turn car's inside lights off first.

Note any cars which circle offices of Freedom Houses. Take license numbers of all suspicious cars. Note make, model, and

---

* The policeman's version of this *Manual* is Colonel Rex Applegate's *Crowd and Riot Control* (Harrisburg, Pa., Stackpole, 1965).

† These are based on the Council of Federated Organizations' *Security Handbook,* issued in June, 1964.

year. Cars without license plates should be reported at once
to the project office.

Domicile

If it can be avoided, try not to sleep near open windows.
Sleep at the back of houses, that is, the part farthest from the
road or street.

Do not stand in doorways at night with lights on behind
you. Draw shades if you sit in lighted rooms. Do not congregate
in front of the house. Make sure doors to houses have locks
and are kept locked.

Keep records of all suspicious events, e.g., cars circling
around the house or office. If an incident occurs, or seems about
to occur, call the project, and also notify local FBI and police.

Under some circumstances it may be advisable for new personnel to make themselves known to local police, introduce
themselves, and tell them their reason for being in the area.

A telephone should be installed. If a private phone is used,
put a lock on it; otherwise, install a pay phone.

Personal

Carry identification at all times. Men should carry draft cards.

All drivers should have in their possession driver's licenses,
registration papers, and bills of sale. The information should also
be on record with the project director. If you are carrying supplies, it is well to have a letter authorizing the supplies from
a particular individual, in order to avoid charges of carrying
stolen goods.

You must not drink in offices or Freedom Houses. This is
especially important for persons under 21.

Avoid bizarre or provocative clothing, and beards. Be neat.

Make sure that medicines prescribed for you by a physician
are clearly marked with your name and the doctor's name, etc.

Police

Under no circumstances should you give the address of the
local person with whom you are living, his or her name, or the

names of any local persons who are associated with you. When police ask where you live, give your local project or Freedom House address, or if necessary your out-of-state home address.

Visitors

Find out who strangers are. If persons come into project offices to "look around," try to find out who they are and what exactly they want to know. All offers of help should be cleared through the project director.

Records

Any written record of any importance should have at least four copies. Bear in mind that offices may be raided at any time. Keep a record of interference with phone lines and of calls to the FBI. This information should go to headquarters.

General

People who do not adhere to disciplinary requirements will be asked to leave the project.

Security is a matter of group responsibility. Each individual should take an interest in every other individual's safety, well-being, and discipline.

At all times you should be aware of dangers to local inhabitants. White volunteers must be especially aware of this point.

9 / ARREST AND THE COURTS

ARREST *

Arrest is taking a person into custody for some official purpose, generally so that he may be held to answer for a crime. If you are arrested, you have rights which protect you from unfair pressure, whether or not you are innocent. What are your rights? Immediately, you have the right to ask the policeman why he is arresting you.

There are three kinds of crimes for which you might be arrested in most states. *Felony* is the most serious. Less serious violations are called *misdemeanors,* and the least serious are *summary offenses.* A policeman does not need a warrant to arrest you for a felony if he sees you commit it, or try to commit it, or if he has reason to believe that a felony has been committed and has reason to think you did it. A policeman does not need a warrant to arrest you if he sees you commit a misdemeanor or summary offense. In many states he must have a warrant to arrest you for a misdemeanor or summary offense he did *not* see you commit.

A *warrant* is an order signed by a justice of the peace or a magistrate (as they are called in some states) or judge. It is made on a complaint by someone. An arrest warrant charges that you committed a crime. The warrant must list the charge against you. It must also direct the policeman to make the arrest and to bring you before a justice of the peace, magistrate, or judge. If you refuse to admit an officer, he may break open a door or a window to serve a warrant.

Generally a policeman must have a search warrant before he

* This and the following two sections are adapted from the Philadelphia ACLU leaflet *If You Are Arrested,* and are included here by courtesy of the Philadelphia Chapter, American Civil Liberties Union.

can search your home. The search warrant must describe the premises to be searched and the thing to be searched for. But of course if you consent to a search without warrant, it is legal.

Even if you think you are not guilty, it is a crime to resist an officer who arrests you legally. If you resist a lawful arrest, a policeman can use all necessary force to arrest you. If you think your rights have been violated by the police, you should consult a lawyer about legal remedies.

AT THE STATION HOUSE

After you are arrested you will be taken to a police station, where a record of your arrest and the charge against you must be reported without unnecessary delay in the "arrest book." Before questioning you the police must tell you the charge. In many places police have the right to fingerprint and photograph you.

You have the right to telephone your family or a friend or an attorney soon after you arrive in the station house and have been booked. In some places police must let you speak over the police phone if you have no money to use a pay phone. (You should always have some dimes and several telephone numbers with you in case some of those you try to call are not in.) You must be given an itemized receipt for all money and property taken from you when booked.

It is your right, under the Constitution, to refuse to say anything that may be used against you later. After giving the police your name, you may not be forced to answer any questions or sign any paper about a crime. A uniformed policeman, a plain-clothesman, or anyone else may not force you to do this. If force or threats are used against you, you should report the fact to your organization or attorney. You may not be forced to take a lie detector test, and you should not ask to take one without having consulted with your attorney.

After arrest and booking you must be taken before a magistrate or judge without unnecessary delay—usually within a day. If you are charged with a felony or a misdemeanor such as larceny, conspiracy to incite a riot, etc., the magistrate or justice of the peace does *not* decide whether you are guilty or innocent. He only decides whether there is a reasonable basis for believing you committed the crime. If he thinks there is a reasonable basis, he will hold you for court. If you are charged with a summary offense, such as disorderly conduct or disturbing the peace, the justice of the peace or the judge himself will decide the case. He will either discharge you or find you guilty.

In any kind of case before a magistrate or justice of the peace, you have the right to (1) be represented by a lawyer, (2) be told exactly what the charge against you is, (3) hear witnesses in support of the charge, and (4) refuse to speak at all.

In summary offense cases, which the justice of the peace himself decides, you have *additional* rights. (1) The J.P. must ask you whether you plead guilty or innocent. (2) You may tell your side of the story if you wish. (3) You may have your own witnesses. (4) If the J.P. finds you guilty he must tell you exactly what you have been found guilty of, and exactly what the penalty is. If you are denied any of these rights and are fined or imprisoned, you have grounds for having the conviction reversed.

APPLYING FOR BAIL

If the J.P. holds you for court (for a more serious offense), you have the right to be allowed to apply promptly for bail. Bail permits you to be released from jail if an amount of money or other security is deposited with the proper official to make sure you will appear in court. The magistrate will fix the amount of bail you must put up. The amount must be reasonable. If it is excessive, your lawyer may ask a higher court to reduce the bail. On very serious felonies, such as murder, robbery, etc., the J.P. is frequently not permitted to set bail, but a higher judge may do so. Bondsmen are often used when you or your family or the organization cannot put up the bail.

It is a good idea to have a lawyer with you when you are taken before a magistrate or a J.P., if only to minimize the risks to you and to raise objections which may be the basis of future appeals. You should ask for a postponement of the hearing if a lawyer satisfactory to you has not been obtained.

In some places, especially in the South, it is wise to sign a statement in advance authorizing someone to retain a lawyer for you. Otherwise even your own lawyer may not be permitted to see you.

THE REALITIES

All these rights are obviously hypothetical. First of all, rights vary widely from state to state. Secondly, your rights are only as good as the willingness of the authorities in any situation to permit you to have them. Law enforcement agencies, particularly (though not exclusively by any means) in the South, need constantly to be reminded that such rights exist, and that they exist for everybody, regardless of race, social class, or sex. Therefore the above outline should not be taken as "legal advice" but rather as a guideline to what *should* happen in a general way when you are arrested.

The U.S. Commission on Civil Rights has regularly detailed instance after instance of the deprivation of persons' constitutional rights, as well as the failure of police to protect persons asserting their constitutional rights. (See its reports for 1959, 1961, and 1963.) In addition, many local ordinances and state laws have been passed especially to control civil rights demonstrations (some have been overturned on appeal to the federal courts). A realistic view would therefore be that constitutional rights are an extremely relative matter, and that in many instances involving civil rights activity, the civil rights worker may as well forget they exist. As the U.S. Civil Rights Commission concluded in 1961 (and certainly there is little evidence to suggest improvement since), "police brutality in the United States today is a serious and continuing problem in many parts of the country. . . . Negroes feel the brunt of official brutality proportionally more than any other group . . . approximately two out of every three complaints (received by the Department of Justice) originated in the 17 Southern states and the District of Columbia. . . ." Nevertheless persons arrested should go through the formality of trying to obtain their rights for appeals purposes.

Most violations charged to civil rights workers will be settled within a state court system. The procedure outlined above applies to state criminal court structures. The federal or U.S. system is different and separate. Unless you violate a law passed by Congress you will rarely find yourself in federal court. Civil rights matters that wind up in federal courts are *usually* matters involving violations of injunctions granted by a federal district court (there are eighty-six districts), or appeals from state supreme courts to the U.S. Supreme Court. There are a variety of federal laws which support civil rights (see Appendices D and E), but it must be remembered that Federal District Court judges are appointed by the President on generally political grounds, and that both judges and juries in federal cases reflect local prejudices more often than not. In addition, the FBI has been notoriously lax in stepping in to help civil rights demonstrators, even when brutality against demonstrators was proceeding right in front of the agents. (For further details on the structure of court systems, different types of law, and the relationship of the judiciary to the legislative and executive branches of state and federal government, consult any standard introductory political science textbook.)

LAW ENFORCEMENT (see also Chapters 8 and 10)

The first thing to remember is that the enforcement of law in this country is extremely inconsistent. Consistency begins to develop only as state and federal authorities step into a local situation. What are some of the inconsistencies which must be kept in mind?

Injunctions by local, state, and federal authorities may be applied against the movement. An injunction is a court order which forbids a certain type of activity (a boycott, picketing, interfering with school integration) or orders a certain type of activity (to obey the law, to register a voter, to maintain the peace). Violations of injunctions result, generally, in quicker punishment because they involve a "contempt of court" proceeding which can be handled quite fast. Thus leaders can quickly be imprisoned and gotten out of the way.

Local enforcement policy sometimes shifts erratically. In many Southern and some Northern communities, police policy is to stay pretty much out of the Negro community altogether, giving the impression of a lack of enforcement; but when violations take place by Negroes outside their community (civil rights demonstrations, for example), there is a crack-down out of all proportion to the danger of the activity. In many Northern communities, on the other hand, police will often protect demonstrators and pickets, but sometimes, without apparent reason, they will take extreme measures against demonstrators, almost as if the police had panicked. This may be because a larger demonstration has brought police into the picture who have no training in "human relations," or who resent this type of duty, or who have become frightened by what they see as a possible

danger to them. Police officers, after all, also reflect local prejudices rather closely.

Do not assume that because an officer is a Negro he is also
a sympathizer. Some Negro police officers "lean over backwards"
to be tough.

PREPARING FOR CIVIL DISOBEDIENCE

Nowadays there is no excuse for civil rights "leaders" to call
a demonstration without carefully planning the consequences.
There is no excuse for shrugging off questions from potential
participants, saying, "Don't worry about it, if it happens, it happens." Leaders owe to participants, and followers have the right
to demand from leaders, the following kinds of information:

(1) Why are we demonstrating? What are our specific demands? Is our demonstration communicating our demands and
putting pressure primarily on those who are responsible for
our troubles?

(2) At what point will it be right to complete or call off the
demonstration? Do we demonstrate for the sake of blowing off
steam, or do we demonstrate to have an effect?

(3) Are we likely to be arrested? If so, what measures have
been taken to make sure some leadership remains outside? What
measures have been taken to make sure some leadership goes
inside to lead activities inside jail?

(4) Will we accept bail? What are the pros and cons of
accepting bail? If we accept bail, what arrangements have been
made for the posting of cash, property, or other security? If we
do not accept bail, what point are we making? Some demonstrations almost inevitably, by their "civil disobedience" nature,
will result in arrest. It is sometimes fruitful to fill the jails in
order to make the point that the cause of the arrest is unjust.
Is this one of those occasions?

(5) If arrest and bail are decided on, what shall be the priority of being released? (Students taking exams, and workers
whose incomes are needed to support families, first).

(6) How much cooperation are we to extend to the police?

What are the pros and cons of going limp? * Shall we sacrifice our dignified appearance (which has public relations value and maintains a certain personal worth) in order to refuse cooperation with an unjust situation?

(7) Have we announced our intention of breaking the law in advance (where that is appropriate, e.g., in Northern communities where arrest is more likely to come only upon the breaking of a definite law, and after warning)? A prior announcement helps to clarify to the community your honesty of purpose and seriousness of intent. In some situations such an announcement will warn the police and they will try to deny you access to the place of the demonstration (e.g., a building). "Sneaking in" has some handicaps, and you might still be able to confront the authorities outside (possibly sitting down there). On the other hand, sometimes the demonstration, to make its point, must be at the particular place; have we discussed the relative merits of this issue?

(8) The question of paying *fines* at the magistrate's court, justice of the peace court, or higher court hearings should also be discussed in advance of any action likely to lead to arrest. The alternative to paying fines is imprisonment for a specified length of time ("thirty days or $100"). Bail is security for your appearance later in court, hence is in a sense only a *loan* to the power structure, which must be paid back. But a fine is lost to you and the movement forever, and furthermore helps to pay the power structure's expenses in running a police force, a prison system, segregated schools, etc. Should you contribute to this by paying fines? This must be weighed against even greater losses in wages for some people if they stay in jail. Again, we do not want to answer this question for you but only advocate that it be intelligently discussed in advance. Obviously, in a "jail-in,"

* "Going limp" is just what the phrase implies. It is a relaxation of all of the body in a kind of physical non-cooperation with the situation, so that the non-cooperator has to be dragged or carried to wherever authorities want him moved. It can be modified by putting hands in pockets, or in situations of violence by folding up (as in football) and covering up the head and other sensitive areas with your arms.

that is, a concentrated attempt to communicate the evil of a law by having masses of people break it and undergo unmerited suffering, it would be foolish to accept bail, or, later, pay fines. The suffering is what communicates, not the paying.

(9) Will we take legal action against officials who rough us up or otherwise molest us in the course of a demonstration? An attorney should clarify to the group what is involved in such a decision; but the final decision should be yours, not his. Some have said that personal actions against officers who, after all, only reflect a generally evil situation, do not help. On the other hand, it should be made clear to officials that you will not tolerate the illegal enforcement of law. In many cases of brutality it will become necessary for you to document the charges by making out a paper called an "affidavit." You should therefore be clear as to exactly what happened, to whom, and by whom. This should include police officers' badge numbers, what kind of police (sheriffs or county, local police, state police, etc.), physical descriptions. You should try to write down what happened as soon as possible, because people's memories, especially under pressure, play tricks.

Your attitude toward the police can contribute to creating a new and better situation. Politeness is often disarming. The polite but firm use of "sir" helps convince the police that you have a regard for them as human beings; it also tells them you will not be bullied.

While we do not seek, here, to give final answers on these many points, we do want to make the point that answers should be arrived at before the demonstration begins. First, it will create a higher sense of morale, because participants will know better what to expect and will feel that the leadership is being responsible and responsive to them. Second, it will educate participants as to the principles and purposes of a demonstration. Any participant may find himself a spokesman, if not in a public situation such as a trial, then later at home in the community. Educated participants are agents for the growth of the movement. Participants who simply follow the leader are sheep to be misled by every orator who comes down the street.

10 / JAIL

In any demonstration likely to lead to violence or arrest, some precautions can be taken which will make life easier. Wear loose clothing in order not to be choked when dragged. Wear decent, tough clothing, but not your best. If you expect to be jailed, wear two sets of underclothes so that you can wear one set while washing the other. This is also helpful padding if you are dragged about by police. An extra pair of socks also helps. Wear a sweater or trenchcoat—cells get cold, and the coat will help cover your legs or serve as a pillow. Take a bunch of kleenex or toilet paper in case that commodity is not available right away. You will probably not be permitted to keep a razor anyhow, but a toothbrush, deodorant, soap, cigarettes, pencil stubs, note paper, ballpoint pen refills (not as bulky as the pen itself), and small books are sometimes permitted, or can be successfully retained, especially during arrests involving many people at one time. Don't forget to ask for a receipt if anything is taken from you.

Do not wear loafers or other loose shoes which you may lose if you are dragged. Girls should not wear high heels. Sharp objects (such as sharpened pencils, pins, brooches) should not be carried or worn.

Make sure you have been to the toilet shortly before the beginning of any demonstration. Make sure you have several dimes and telephone numbers with you, and that someone on the outside knows you may be going to jail.

For those who wear eyeglasses: carry a hard case to protect your glasses when trouble appears imminent. If you absolutely must wear glasses, carry adhesive tape, and fix three strips vertically across your glasses, one in front of each ear, and one down your forehead, across the bridge of your glasses, and down your nose.

VARIETIES OF JAILS

It is hard to generalize about the kinds of places actionists are put—city and county jails, open stockades, and garages are used. The county jail often has four grades of accommodations: dormitories (minimum security), unlocked cells opening on a common area or cell block (medium security), locked cells (maximum security), and cells for "solitary," generally without windows, often called "the hole." Wherever you are put you will usually find a rather dull routine, starting early in the morning until early in the evening. In spite of the idleness, there is a good deal of tension where people are locked in, and this tension can be the greatest hardship of a jail period.

INMATES

The inmates already there for other offenses are often curious about you and can be your allies in conflicts with prison officials. In one county prison the other inmates, white and Negro, conducted a sit-down strike to back up the demands of the demonstrators that their cell doors be unlocked during the day.

James Farmer recalls another dramatic example of this tactic: "I remember one night at the jail, a voice called up from the cell block beneath us, where other Negro prisoners were housed. 'Upstairs!' the anonymous prisoner shouted. We replied, 'Downstairs!' 'Upstairs!' replied the voice, 'Sing your freedom song.' And the Freedom Riders sang. We sang old folk songs and gospel songs to which new words had been written, telling of the Freedom Ride and its purpose. Then the downstairs prisoners, whom the jailers had said were our enemies, sang for us." *

KEEPING UP MORALE

Sometimes exhausted civil rights workers look forward to jail as a place where they can catch up on their sleep. This is one important use of jail, but in general other methods must

* Quoted in Guy and Candie Carawan, *We Shall Overcome!* New York, Oak Publications, 1963.

be found to lick the great enemy of morale—idleness. There are a number of things which bolster morale and use up the time, such as singing. Many freedom songs were born in prison, and anyone can make up new verses to the songs you know. Singing brings a sense of solidarity and hope, and also helps to relieve tension.

An extremely important thing you can do is teaching: prisoners often devise homemade lectures, do role-playing, and have discussions of nonviolence and direct action. Nearly everyone knows something the others do not—prison can be a time for sharing and learning. George Bernard Shaw is supposed to have said, "I'd rather go to jail than to school." Make sure to put any teachers or professors who may be with you to full use.

You may be able to think up projects which contribute to prison life, such as producing a prison newspaper. Some SNCC workers were publicized in newspapers and radio broadcasts when they had a project of painting their jail cells. In addition to fighting restlessness and providing short-term goals to shoot for, such projects can demonstrate the basically constructive attitude which the freedom movement is building.

GUARDS

It may be hard for you to think of some guards as people, but it may be hard for them to think of you that way too. Keep in mind that they are there to do a job, and protests should be reserved for situations when guards are harsh, rather than when they are simply carrying out duties.

Marilyn Eisenberg recalls: "Our matron, a formidable looking woman from Alabama, was at first very rough with the girls. She rarely spoke, and although we thought she was sympathetic to us as prisoners, we were sure she hated us as Freedom Riders. But some of the girls, in the true nonviolent spirit, saw her as a human being and not as a symbol of authority and oppression. Little by little they began to speak to her. At first it was just 'good morning' or 'thank you,' and then we began to joke with her and have longer and longer conversations. Before I left Parchman she was singing for us on our make-believe radio programs and was often heard humming our freedom songs." *

AGITATION INSIDE THE JAIL

Many persons when they go to jail take the attitude of Gandhi—that jail is not a grim necessity so much as an honorable service for the cause. If Gandhi broke the law, even an unjust law, he willingly accepted the punishment. This is why it is called *civil* disobedience rather than *criminal* disobedience.

But Gandhi felt that if the prisoner's dignity was being trampled on and his rights as a prisoner being violated, resistance inside prison became a duty. In India prisoners sometimes refused to cooperate with the guards as a means of correcting wrongs.

One of the common ways civil rights actionists, as well as regular prisoners, demonstrate inside a prison is by noise-making. Spoons are hit against the bars, there is yelling, and shoes are pounded on the walls until the authorities make the concession asked for, or until the prisoners are exhausted. While noise-making is sometimes effective, it is not well suited to maintaining a nonviolent discipline and can get out of control and become a riot, with windows being smashed and prisoners and guards getting hurt.

Another method of demonstrating is to conduct sit-downs when outside the cell or when moving from one place to another. An important precaution here is that you should relax your body as much as possible, for tissue can be damaged and torn when you are lifted or dragged if your muscles are tensed.

A third method is the hunger strike. Generally, prisoners engaging in a hunger strike drink water; not to do so is fatal in ten to fifteen days unless there is intravenous injection or force-feeding. Some fasts taking only water have lasted two months or more. Fasting in jail can be a powerful means of protesting prison evils such as segregation. Officials do not like to have deaths occur in their institutions.

Total non-cooperation is an extension of the hunger strike.

* In *We Shall Overcome!* New York, Oak Publications, 1963.

This involves an absolute refusal to cooperate in any way what-
soever with the prison system, including refusal to eat, drink,
move, get up, dress or undress, or go to the toilet. Non-
cooperation to this degree is extremely dangerous since it forces
authorities to force-feed, and otherwise physically handle, the
prisoner. It requires a great deal of courage on the part of the
non-cooperator, and in turn can command deep respect on the
part of the jailers after a while, if the prisoner maintains his
good will toward the jailers. Both hunger strikes and total non-
cooperation have been practiced by conscientious objectors to
the military draft in this country, and one such effort resulted
in the unconditional release of the prisoner, but only after
months of suffering on his part.

SUGGESTED RULES FOR PRISON *

1. A Freedom Army recruit should be a model prisoner.
2. Accept jail discipline and its hardships. It's supposed to
be rough. It's not supposed to be a picnic.
3. Always act and speak with honesty.
4. Cooperate with prison officials and don't break prison
rules unless they are against dignity and self-respect or our
principles.
5. You may protest and refuse food served insultingly or
uncleanly.
6. Do all jobs to the best of your ability.
7. Do not hesitate to ask for essential spiritual and physical
needs, but do not be irritated if you do not get them.
8. Don't take part in improper joking with prison officials.
9. Don't bother trustees and guards with unnecessary errands
or ask special privileges and favors.
10. Make no distinction between demonstrators and ordinary prisoners.
11. Ask no favors and claim no privileges which ordinary
prisoners do not get and which you do not need except for
maintaining health.

* Based on Southern Christian Leadership Conference, *Handbook for Freedom
Army Recruits* (pamphlet).

12. Remember that guards are human beings and try to treat them as such. Have regard for fellow prisoners and do not be selfish.

13. Do nothing to demoralize your fellow prisoners. Take responsibility for keeping everyone in good spirits. Do not take part in teasing or conversation that might hurt feelings or start a fight.

11 / NONVIOLENCE AND ARMED DEFENSE

In recent years a sense of desperation has grown in the Negro community. This desperation is rooted in the failure of the civil rights movement to achieve, and of the white power structure to surrender, satisfactory gains. The result has been a significant growth of organizations such as, on the one extreme, the Muslims (Black Separatism), and on the other extreme more traditional integrationist groupings which are non-affiliated, tend to be emotional in their tone, and seem reluctant or unable to discuss, advocate, or train followers in nonviolence. There has been an increase in attacks on the concepts and tactics of nonviolence, an increasing interest in the tactics of armed defense, and a higher incidence of semi-political, violent outbursts in the Negro community.

Healthy debate between these two important tendencies in direct action (nonviolence versus armed defense) has been rare. Respected leaders of nonviolent groups have been reluctant to publicize the opposition, and the advocates of armed defense generally do not care about white public opinion, and thus have limited their propaganda work to Negro circles. But healthy debate is essential if we are to understand the two tendencies, and if we are to have an accurate perspective on civil rights in the next few years.

Advocates of various brands of Black Nationalism and armed defense (they overlap, but are not synonymous) criticize nonviolence on these general grounds:

Argument 1: Nonviolence does not look out for the safety and life of individuals. Leaders of nonviolent movements talk in terms of spilling "our" blood, rather than spilling "theirs." This is nonsense. Why should the innocents be made to suffer? Who are these leaders, to be willing to sacrifice their followers to racist madmen? It is important to safeguard our lives and the lives of our families. Nonviolence cannot do this because it does nothing to deter violence from mobs, police authorities, etc. In order to avoid many kinds of direct violence against innocent Negroes, and in order to avoid violent reprisals against civil rights demonstrators, it is necessary to make sure potential attackers understand that the price of attack will be high. In many instances, notably in Monroe, North Carolina, "deterrence theory" has paid off. Knowledge that Negroes are armed and will defend themselves deters aggression.

Rebuttal: In any direct action campaign where the opponents are determined, campaigners will suffer. This is the experience of history, whether the strategy is violent or nonviolent. The cost of social change is often high and the brunt of it has often been taken by those who have the most to gain from the change.

The real question is not, "How can the suffering be avoided?" The question is, "How can it be *minimized?*" In case after case the violent strategy has brought more suffering to the innocent than the nonviolent strategy. This is even true on a national level —compare the freedom struggles of India and Kenya, against the same British power. The nonviolent Indians lost fewer lives and had fewer injured than the Mao Mao movement of Kenya, despite the fact that the Indian movement was larger and lasted longer.

Violence does not deter violence in the long run, and often not even in the short run. Again and again in the civil rights struggle police have been itching to shoot into demonstrations but have not fired because they could not find the excuse of "self-defense" or "rioting." Sometimes in nonviolent struggles the rulers have sent spies into the movement to start violence so they would have an excuse to mow the campaigners down.

The argument for violence in self-defense assumes that the opponents are more afraid of violence than of nonviolence. This

may be true of individual policemen, but it is not true of their bosses. Violence is what police and armies know how to deal with—they are experienced in this. What baffles them is the use of disciplined nonviolence—they actually do not know what to do with it. Imagine 1,000 Negroes in Birmingham setting up barricades and shooting it out after extreme provocation—this is simply war, and the government has won bigger wars than this! A thousand Negroes, however, *have* demonstrated in Birmingham for several months without being put down. Nonviolence is simply harder to handle, and if your job is to preserve the status quo, you will be more afraid of it.

In short, then, nonviolent action actually prevents more bloodshed and deters brutality better than violence does. If however, you are looking for a 100 percent guaranteed safe way of action, then you do not belong in a dynamic struggle for social change. Freedom is not free.

Argument 2: Nonviolence drains the potential militancy of the Negro community by giving a theory of change which is an illusion. Nonviolence may be "nice," and can win the approval of *parts* of the white power structure, but it can never mount the kind of attack on the power structure that will be necessary to win. The moment that kind of attack is mounted, reprisals will be fierce, and the Negroes, unused to defending themselves, will become disillusioned, apathetic, or will be killed.

Rebuttal: The answer to this lies in the history of the last ten years. It was nonviolent leadership which taught Montgomery Negroes in 1956 that they must struggle for their freedom, that no one could *give* it to them. The significant militant movements in terms of mass support and gains have been nonviolent. It is strange reasoning which sees the thousands of Negroes now involved in the civil rights struggle who were not involved before as an example of "drained militancy."

Argument 3: Nonviolence does not make sense in this country, and particularly in the Negro community. This nation is based on a tradition of armed struggle against oppression: Lexington and Concord, the slave uprisings, the raid on Harpers Ferry were all in the American tradition. Nonviolence is foreign to this nation's ways of doing things. Furthermore, the heart of the Negro community itself (especially the urban slum ghetto) is used to violence. Negroes have for centuries been the victims of violence, and this has become a part of their way of life. Nonviolence is a tactic of the white middle class intellectual, not of the Negro working class. Ultimately, it violates the "survival common sense" of the Negro urban masses.

Rebuttal: If this statement were true it would not be very important, for any way of life must have new elements introduced constantly in order to remain vigorous and alive. But in fact, it is not true.

The roots of nonviolent action in America go back to Puritan Massachusetts and to colonial Pennsylvania. The nonviolent technique of the boycott was used during the American Revolution and before. The history of the labor movement in this country is full of the use of nonviolent tactics, sometimes alongside violence but often not.

Our way of life includes some standards which go better with nonviolence than with violence. We say we believe in respecting the dignity of the human personality, we say we believe in the Golden Rule and in brotherhood. The Christian ethic, certainly a part of the American heritage (and that of the Negro working class), tells us to overcome evil with good.

Argument 4: Racism is a disease, a product of diseased minds. The violence of racism cannot be dealt with by the rational thought processes and procedures (intended to "convert" the racist) of nonviolence. It is far less important to "convert" the racist enemy than it is to remove his opposition to our struggle, and eliminate his threat to our homes and families. This can be done by restraining him physically, for while armed defense may not convert him, he is still rational enough to understand that action on his part will result in instantaneous punishment. Would the church in Birmingham have been bombed if it had been well understood that ten prominent racists would suffer assassination as punishment?

Rebuttal: Nonviolent action does *not* work primarily on the rational level. If discussion and reasoning were enough to convert segregationists, nonviolent action would not be necessary. It is because the power of logic is not enough that nonviolent action was devised, for nonviolence brings three more kinds of power: economic power, political power, psychological power.

Economic power has already been discussed under strategy and tactics. Using arms in self-defense adds nothing to this power.

Political power makes it difficult for the politicians to rule without making concessions. Mass demonstrations are powerful on this level: they make it appear that the politicians are not in control. This is why demonstrations are often attacked even though they do not seem to be threatening anything. Using arms in self-defense adds nothing to this power, since it only relieves the authorities of some of their difficulties in repressing the demonstrations.

Psychological power has converted some racists and has moved many moderates closer to the civil rights struggle. Using violence would detract seriously from this power. The organized religious bodies of this country may not be involved as much as we think they should be in the struggle for change, but would they be involved even as much as they are if the movement had been violent? Allies *are* needed, for Negroes involved in civil rights remain a very small minority; the nonviolent movement forces right-minded people to confront the real issues of social justice. Were the movement violent, many people would evade the real issue of justice by getting "hung up" on the violent *means*. Riots give people an excuse they've been looking for. Nonviolence gives them no excuses—they've got to take a stand on the real issue.

A final point on the question of racism and diseased minds: psychiatrists in progressive mental hospitals now use nonviolence rather than violent physical repression with the mentally ill because they find it heals better.*

Argument 5: It may be that nonviolence is the best way. It may be that violence serves only to divert attention from the fact that the real struggle also involves the kinds of social and economic issues that can't be settled by violence, and that require allies (for example, the struggle of both Negroes and whites for jobs in an era of increasing automation). It may be that nonviolence requires a greater courage than violence. But I haven't got that kind of courage. I'm not ready to be that pure, and neither are most of the activists in the movement.

---

* For further explanation of how this psychological power works, see George Lakey, *Nonviolent Action: How It Works*, Pendle Hill Pamphlets, Wallingford, Pennsylvania, 1963.

If I am living with a Negro farmer and he keeps a rifle in his closet and is prepared to use it to protect himself, his home, and his family against night raiders, I'm not prepared to tell him not to use it, or to sit it out while he uses it. Maybe nonviolence has a psychological power that arms don't have—but armed resistance to evil in a situation where nonviolence has become, for whatever reason, irrelevant, is better than no resistance at all. And dying with a chance of survival because you're fighting back is better than certain death by bombs and bullets in the night.

Rebuttal: If nonviolent direct action is the strongest weapon the civil rights worker has, then he should not let himself be put into a position where it is almost impossible to use. When the worker lives with the gun-toting farmer he is obviously going to have trouble using nonviolence successfully. In military campaigns an effective weapon can still be defeated if accompanied by poor tactics. Each strategy of power, nonviolent or violent, has its own requirements, and no one can act effectively without paying attention to those requirements.

One of the requirements of nonviolence is that, to be most effective, it must be clear. The power of nonviolence grows the more it is the clear policy of the whole group, and not confused by elements of violence.

As Robert Moses, head of the Mississippi 1964 Summer Project, put it, "One reason we've survived is that we haven't had guns and everyone knew it."

Now if, in spite of the worker's efforts, he is caught in a situation where most of the people are using violence, his decision goes back to his own philosophy. As far as nonviolence is concerned, he is caught "with both hands behind his back." However, he is not facing "certain death" if he will not use violence, for as Quakers showed on the American frontier, the best way to survive can still be the way of nonviolence. And if it is a question of whether to die using violence or nonviolence, each person must ask which will give his death most meaning for the cause and for his God.

Argument 6: Finally, when push comes to shove, the power structure will be ruthless in defending its privileges. Nonviolence is all very well when there is not much at stake—a cup of coffee, a few votes between tweedledum and tweedledee, a handful of jobs. But when it comes to votes in areas where Negroes form large proportions of the population (and by their nature as workers and poor farmers could create a social revolution through the ballot box); when it comes to *real* numbers of jobs, housing, schools; when the Negro movement begins to march upon the *real* citadels of the power elite, then no mercy will be shown, and we will be crushed despite all the protestations of Christian love. Only arms will save us.

Rebuttal: If this argument means that the only way 170,000,-000 whites will give up their key privileges is for 20,000,000 Negroes to defeat them with arms, then there is no hope. Obviously, Negroes with .22 rifles, dynamite, and Molotov Cocktails are not going to defeat tanks, planes, and overwhelming numbers, despite any temporary dislocations they may cause. Trying this guerrilla-type terrorist activity will bring only terror, hardship, and death, and most of that to Negro families who are innocent of actual involvement in these romantic but bloody military adventures.

Fortunately, we have seen this argument before and know something of its validity. Workers in this country were once told that only violent revolution would accomplish real gains, that the ruling class in America would not willingly give up enough to allow for a decent wage and decent working conditions. As we know, this was false, for the workers found a means of struggle which enabled them to apply pressure and *still* attract allies in church and government. The labor movement might be in better shape today if it had been more principled in its devotion to brotherhood and nonviolence, but even so workers accomplished much of what believers in violence said was impossible.

More important than the reasons for the impracticality of

a policy of armed defense, though, is the way a man looks at himself. Does he want to bring into a moral revolution the use of immoral means? Does he want personally to fall into the trap of saying, "That man is not my brother, is not even a human being, is worthy of my contempt and my bullet"? The surest way of encouraging evil to spread is to let it engulf your own heart.

Appendix A
A NOTE ON FURTHER READING

The Negro in America has undergone centuries of oppression. He has been robbed of his manhood and his history. It is important, in order to restore the self-worth of an individual, that he have some sense of who he is and of his past. Continuing ignorance of Negro history at the high school and college level contributes to maintaining prejudiced views of Negroes by whites, and undermines the Negro's self-esteem. As the anthropologist Melville J. Herskovits pointed out in his excellent *The Myth of the Negro Past* (Boston, Beacon Press, 1958), "the American Negro, in discovering that he has a past, has added assurance that he will have a future." Workers therefore owe it to themselves to become familiar with Negro history, and to transmit what they learn to both whites and Negroes. The purpose of this appendix is to suggest some good sources on this neglected subject.

The history of Negro protest is old. On the West African slave ships, West Indies, and pre-Civil War South period, see Herskovits (cited above) and Herbert Aptheker's *Negro Slave Revolts in the United States, 1526-1860* (New York, International Publishers, 1939). On the Reconstruction period and the era of agrarian discontent (roughly, to 1896), a handy and well-written work is C. Vann Woodward's *The Strange Career of Jim Crow* (New York, Oxford University Press, 1955), or see his longer, more scholarly *Origins of the New South* (Baton Rouge, Louisiana State University Press, 1951). After the collapse of Populism, disillusionment and apathy characterized Negro political and social life. The non-political nature of the period was symbolized by the philosophy of Booker T. Washington. August Meier analyzes this epoch in *Negro Thought in America, 1880-1915* (Ann Arbor, University of Michigan Press, 1963). This era was quickly followed by the Niagara Movement and the founding of the NAACP by W. E. B. DuBois and others—see his *Dusk of Dawn* (New York, Harcourt, Brace, 1940), or the paperback *The Souls of Black Folk* (New York, Crest, 1964), or the biography by Francis L. Broderick, *W. E. B. DuBois: Negro Leader in a Time of Crisis* (Stanford, Stanford University Press, 1959).

The turn of the century marked the beginning of large-scale migrations of Southern Negroes into Northern cities. Good background material is to be found in the superb volume by W. J. Cash, *The Mind of the South* (New York, Knopf, 1941). The development of the urban political machine is discussed in Drake and Cayton's *Black Metropolis* (New York, Harcourt, Brace, 1945) and in Harold F. Gosnell's *Negro Politicians* (Chicago, University of Chicago Press, 1935)—both are about Chicago. A different view which casts an interesting light on Rep. Adam Clayton Powell's career is his *Marching Blacks* (New York, Dial Press, 1945). A superb analysis of the Negro's potential political power, as well as much essential information about Southern politics in general, is V. O. Key's *Southern Politics in State and Nation* (New York, Knopf, 1950, and Vintage paperback).

With urbanization came trade unionization. A. Philip Randolph's early years are mapped out in Brailsford Brazeal's *The Brotherhood of Sleeping Car Porters* (New York, Harper, 1946), and a more general survey is Herbert R. Northrup's *Organized Labor and the Negro* (New York, Harper, 1944), a bit outdated now.

The disappointments of World War I resulted in a backlash of Negro separatism—the Garvey movement, possibly the largest movement of Negroes in this country to date. Edward D. Cronon's *Black Moses* (Madison, University of Wisconsin Press, 1962) discusses this, and of course the more up-to-date version of this movement is covered by C. Eric Lincoln's *The Black Muslims in America* (Boston, Beacon Press, 1961) and E. U. Essien-Udom's *Black Nationalism* (New York, Dell, 1962). The Communist party, too, advocated a separate state for Negroes, and various turns of party policy can be traced in Wilson Record's *The Negro and the Communist Party* (Chapel Hill, University of North Carolina Press, 1951).

The Negro's cultural contribution to this country should not be neglected in such a historical survey. Of particular interest are the works of Alain Locke, a short survey by Margaret Butcher, *The Negro in American Culture* (New York, Mentor, 1957), the interesting memoir by Roi Ottley, *New World A-Coming* (Boston, Houghton-Mifflin, 1943), and the somewhat more specialized *The Negro Novel in America* (New Haven, Yale University Press, 1958) by Robert Bone. Essential to an understanding of Negro life is a reading of the works of Richard Wright, especially his *Native Son,* Ralph Ellison's *Invisible Man,* and the essays and novels of James Baldwin, particularly *Go Tell It On The Mountain.* The poetry and novels of Langston Hughes are also important as are the works of many, many others. Also see Michael Harrington's important *The Other America* (New York, Penguin, 1963).

The recent period of protest probably began in 1941 with the March On Washington Movement, carefully described by Herbert Garfinkel in *When Negroes March* (Glencoe, Free Press, 1959). The Bible of the movement remains Martin Luther King's description of the Montgomery Bus Boycott, *Stride Toward Freedom* (New York, Harper, 1958). Also see his newly published *Why We Can't Wait* (New York, New American Library, 1964). Two other recent surveys of the current protest are Dan Wakefield's *Revolt in the South* (New York, Evergreen, 1960) which covers the early sit-in period and its background, and Nat Hentoff's *The New Equality* (New York, Viking, 1965), which is more up to date. An alternative course of action (armed defense) is advocated in Robert F. Williams' *Negroes With Guns* (New York, Marzani and Munsell, 1962).

Howard Zinn's *SNCC: The New Abolitionists* (Boston, Beacon Press, 1964) is a must for all students of the current movement.

For those interested in a closer look at problems of community structure, Floyd Hunter's *Community Power Structure* (New York, Anchor, 1953) remains standard. Negro community life is examined in Drake and

Cayton (cited above); John Dollard's *Caste and Class in a Southern Town* (New York, Anchor, 1949) is still good. On the psychological level, Gordon W. Allport's *The Nature of Prejudice* (New York, Anchor, 1958) still leads the field, and for powerful insights into Negro psychology Abram Kardiner and Lionel Ovesey's *The Mark of Oppression* (New York, Meridian, 1962) is extremely interesting. Negro family life is discussed in the standard *Negro Family in the U.S.* (New York, Dryden, 1948) by the Negro scholar E. Franklin Frazier, and also in his well-known *Black Bourgeoisie* (New York, Collier, 1962). A good general text on Negro history is John Hope Franklin's *From Slavery to Freedom* (New York, Knopf, 1957). Arnold Rose's condensation of Gunnar Myrdal's *The American Dilemma* (still a top work in the field), entitled *The Negro in America* (Boston, Beacon Press, 1957), is a good handy reference work. Thomas F. Pettigrew's *A Profile of the Negro American* (Princeton, Van Nostrand, 1964), is one of the best all-round summaries of Negro life.

Not much has yet been written on nonviolence, but Mulford Sibley's anthology, *The Quiet Battle* (Chicago, Quadrangle Books, 1963), is valuable, as is Martin Luther King (cited above). Leo Kuper's *Passive Resistance in South Africa* (New Haven, Yale University Press, 1957) is very good, and Richard B. Gregg's *The Power of Nonviolence* (Nyack, N.Y., Fellowship, 1959 ed.) is a good general discussion of the concept and its ramifications, as is Joan Bondurant's *Conquest of Violence* (Princeton, Princeton University Press, 1959), and William Miller's *Nonviolence: A Christian Interpretation* (New York, Association Press, 1964).

Hadley Cantril's *The Psychology of Social Movements* (New York, Wiley, 1941) has very good material on mob behavior, and Killian and Grigg's *Racial Crisis in America* (New York, Prentice-Hall, 1964) has a solid section on biracial committees and other current matters. Negotiation is covered in Dean and Rosen's *A Manual of Intergroup Relations* (Chicago, University of Chicago Press, 1955). Musically speaking, Guy and Candie Carawan's *We Shall Overcome!* (New York, Oak Publications, 1963) is the comprehensive work. An excellent introduction to what can be expected in jails and other "total institutions" is Erving Goffman's *Asylums,* Part I (New York, Anchor, 1961).

Broderick and Meier's *Negro Protest Thought in the Twentieth Century* (Indianapolis, Bobbs-Merrill, 1965) and Murphy and Elinson's *Problems and Prospects of the Negro Movement* (Belmont, Calif., Wadsworth, 1966) are two good recent anthologies on current developments.

Appendix B
THE BILL OF RIGHTS AND CIVIL RIGHTS

From the first ten amendments to the Constitution of the United States:

Article 1: Congress shall make no law respecting an establishment of religion, or prohibiting the free exercise thereof; or abridging the freedom of speech or of the press; or the right of the people peaceably to assemble, and to petition the government for a redress of grievances.

Article 2: A well-regulated militia being necessary to the security of a free state, the right of the people to keep and bear arms shall not be infringed.

Article 3: No soldier shall, in time of peace, be quartered in any house without the consent of the owner, nor in time of war, but in a manner to be prescribed by law.

Article 4: The right of the people to be secure in their persons, houses, papers, and effects against unreasonable searches and seizures, shall not be violated, and no warrants shall issue but upon probable cause, supported by oath or affirmation and particularly describing the place to be searched, and the person or things to be seized.

Article 5: No person shall be held to answer for a capital or otherwise infamous crime, unless on a presentment or indictment of a grand jury, except in cases arising in the land or naval forces, or in the militia, when in actual service in time of war or public danger; nor shall any person be subject for the same offense to be twice put in jeopardy of life or limb; nor shall be compelled in any criminal case to be a witness against himself, nor be deprived of life, liberty, or property, without due process of law; nor shall private property be taken for public use without just compensation.

Article 6: In all criminal prosecutions the accused shall enjoy the right to a speedy and public trial, by an impartial jury of the state and district wherein the crime shall have been committed, which district shall have previously been ascertained by law, and to be informed of the nature and cause of the accusation; to be confronted with the witnesses against him; to have compulsory process for obtaining witnesses in his favor, and to have the assistance of counsel for his defense.

. . .

Article 8: Excessive bail shall not be required, nor excessive fines imposed, nor cruel and unusual punishment inflicted.

. . .

Appendix C
AMENDMENTS 13, 14, AND 15 TO THE CONSTITUTION OF THE UNITED STATES

Article 13: (Section 1) Neither slavery nor involuntary servitude, except as a punishment for crime whereof the party shall have been duly convicted, shall exist within the United States or any place subject to their jurisdiction.

(Section 2) Congress shall have the power to enforce this article by appropriate legislation.

Article 14: (Section 1) All persons born or naturalized in the United States, and subject to the jurisdiction thereof, are citizens of the United States and of the State wherein they reside. No State shall make or enforce any law which shall abridge the privileges or immunities of citizens of the United States; nor shall any State deprive any person of life, liberty, or property without due process of law; nor deny to any person within its jurisdiction the equal protection of the laws.

(Section 2) Representatives shall be apportioned among the several States according to their respective numbers, counting the whole number of persons in each state, excluding Indians not taxed. But when the right to vote at any election for the choice of electors for President and Vice-President of the United States, Representatives in Congress, the executive and judicial officers of a State, or the members of the legislature thereof, is denied to any of the male [Article 19 now includes female] inhabitants of such State, being twenty-one years of age, and citizens of the United States, or in any way abridged, except for participation in rebellion, or other crime, the basis of representation therein shall be reduced in the proportion which the number of such male citizens shall bear to the number of male citizens twenty-one years of age in such State.

. . .

(Section 5) The Congress shall have power to enforce, by appropriate legislation, the provisions of this article.

Article 15: (Section 1) The right of citizens of the United States to vote shall not be denied or abridged by the United States or by any State on account of race, color, or previous condition of servitude.

(Section 2) The Congress shall have power to enforce this article by appropriate legislation.

Appendix D
THE CIVIL RIGHTS ACT OF 1964

The U.S. Civil Rights Act of 1964 (H.R. 7152), only the third civil rights act passed since Reconstruction (the others were passed in 1957 and 1960 under President Eisenhower), was signed into law on July 2. It consists of eleven titles, or chapters. Following is a brief summary of each of these, indicating what the act is supposed to do, and how various rights are supposed to be secured.

Title I—Voting Rights

Title I amends previous voting rights law (see other sections of this appendix) to eliminate any discriminatory procedures which might bar individuals from registering to vote, or from voting in federal elections. Above all, it prohibits literacy tests unless *everyone* is given such tests, and unless copies of the tests and answers are made available. It is assumed that anyone who has completed the sixth grade of any accredited public or private school is "literate" enough to vote.

The Attorney General of the U.S. may institute a court action in which three federal judges hear the facts in such a case, and decide whether or not there is a pattern of discrimination. If there is, a court order to eliminate the discriminatory practice can be issued.

Title II—Injunctive Relief Against Discrimination in Places of Public Accommodation

This is the "public accommodations" section of the law. It says that in most inns, hotels, motels, or other places of lodging, "All persons shall be entitled to the full and equal enjoyment of the goods, services, facilities, privileges, advantages and accommodations . . ."

The same thing is true of most restaurants, cafeterias, lunchrooms, lunch counters, and soda fountains, as well as most motion picture houses, theaters, concert halls, sports arenas, and stadiums, particularly those which handle goods which travel in interstate commerce (and today most goods at one point or another do). Private clubs are exempt from these provisions, as are some other facilities.

Any person who thinks he has been the victim of such prohibited discrimination, or who thinks he is about to become a victim, may go to federal court and apply for an injunction, a restraining order, or other kinds of civil relief to undo the wrong or prevent the wrong from being done. The U.S. Attorney General may join in the case, or in some situations enter the case alone by requesting a three-judge court to make a finding or grant a court order to overturn or prevent the discriminatory act. The victim or the Attorney General need not wait for local administrative routines to be exhausted before initiating such action.

Title III—Desegregation of Public Facilities

Any person who believes he is being deprived of the equal protection of the law because of race, color, religion, or national origin, because of a denial of equal access to public facilities owned, operated, or managed by a state or a part of a state, can complain in writing to the Attorney General. The Attorney General, if he believes the complaint is just, and if he believes that the complainant cannot himself afford the legal costs of a court action, can himself go to court to try to obtain an appropriate court order or injunction.

Title IV—Desegregation of Public Education

Any time a parent, or group of parents, or an individual student, feel that their children, or the students themselves, are being deprived by a school board of equal protection of the laws, or are being denied admission to a school, or are being forced out of a school (including public colleges) because of race, color, religion, or national origin, they can make a complaint to the U.S. Attorney General in writing. He may then institute a civil suit in federal court and try to get an appropriate court order. However, this does not include court orders requiring "busing" in order to achieve racial balance. Again, the Attorney General must be convinced that the case is just, and that the complainant(s) cannot themselves afford the legal costs involved.

Title V—Commission on Civil Rights

The Civil Rights Act of 1964 continues the life of the U.S. Commission on Civil Rights until 1968. The Commission, while it has no power to enforce any law, or to investigate any private club, fraternity, sorority, or religious organization, may investigate charges that citizens are being deprived of the right to vote, are being deprived of the equal protection of the law, or are being discriminated against in the fields of employment, education, housing, and other public facilities. It is authorized to make reports of its findings and recommendations, including suggestions for changes in the law.

Title VI—Nondiscrimination in Federally Assisted Programs

Nobody may be discriminated against in any program or activity which receives funds from the federal government, nor may anyone be excluded from such programs on account of race, color, or national origin. Federal departments and agencies which grant financial assistance are to issue rules and regulations enforcing this part of the act, such rules and regulations to be approved by the President. Enforcement can be made effective under Title VI by means of ending financial assistance, or refusing to continue or grant financial assistance to recipients who have been found guilty of discriminatory practices in a hearing. Such administrative hearings may be reviewed by the federal courts.

Title VII—Equal Employment Opportunity

No employer (meaning anyone who, in 1965-66, has one hundred or more employees, during 1966-67 has seventy-five or more employees, during 1967-68 has fifty or more employees and after that time twenty-five or more employees), employment agency, or labor union may discriminate against an individual in the process of hiring and firing, wages, conditions of employment, work classifications, or other conditions involving his status as an employee because of race, color, religion, sex, or national origin. Two exceptions to this part of the law are (1) in the case of individuals belonging to subversive organizations and (2) where religion, sex, or national origin is a legitimate occupational qualification.

Apprenticeship, training, and retraining programs are covered by this portion of the act. Advertising relating to employment may not indicate any preferences based on race, color, religion, sex, or national origin unless religion, sex, or national origin is a legitimate qualification for the job.

Title VII creates an Equal Employment Opportunity Commission of five members. The Commission has power to investigate alleged violations of Title VII, and if it believes charges to be true, it has the power to try to eliminate unlawful employment practices by informal means—conference, conciliation, and persuasion. If the Commission fails to get voluntary compliance, any person found by the Commission to be the victim of discrimination may go to court, and if the victim does not have financial resources the court can appoint an attorney and waive fees and costs. If the court then finds that an unlawful employment practice has been engaged in, a court order to correct the wrong will follow.

Title VIII—Registration and Voting Statistics

The Commission on Civil Rights may recommend a registration and voting survey in various geographic areas. Title VIII authorizes the Secretary of Commerce to conduct such surveys when called upon to do so by the Commission.

Title IX—Intervention and Procedure After Removal in Civil Rights Cases

In any court action seeking relief from the denial of equal protection of the laws under the 14th Amendment, or due to race, color, religion, or national origin (see other appendices), the Attorney General may intervene if he believes the case to be of general public importance.

Title X—Establishment of Community Relations Service

Under the act, a Community Relations Service is established under the Department of Commerce. The Service has as its chief job the task of providing assistance to communities in resolving disputes and difficulties as a result of discrimination. It may offer its services to iron out difficulties either on its own initiative, or on the request of state or local officials or other interested persons.

Title XI—Miscellaneous

Any person who is being tried for criminal contempt of court as the result of violating court orders arising from violations of the public accommodations, education, employment, or federal programs sections of this act is entitled to a trial by jury, and upon conviction for contempt of court shall be fined not more than $1,000 or imprisoned not more than six months.

Appendix E
SELECTED CRIMINAL AND CIVIL STATUTES

(Caution: do not attempt to interpret the wording without the aid of an attorney. For further assistance, see Vol. 5, "Justice," of the 1960 U.S. Civil Rights Commission *Report*.)

Title 18, U.S. Criminal Code, Section 241

If two or more persons conspire to injure, oppress, threaten, or intimidate any citizen in the free exercise or enjoyment of any right or privilege secured to him by the Constitution or laws of the United States, or because of his having so exercised the same; or

If two or more persons go in disguise on the highway, or on the premises of another, with intent to prevent or hinder his free exercise or enjoyment of any right or privilege so secured—

They shall be fined not more than $5,000, or imprisoned not more than 10 years, or both.

Title 18, U.S. Criminal Code, Section 242

Whoever, under color of any law, statute, ordinance, regulation, or custom, willfully subjects any inhabitant of any State, Territory, or District to the deprivation of any rights, privileges, or immunities secured or protected by the Constitution or laws of the United States, or to different punishments, pains, or penalties, on account of such inhabitant being an alien, or by reason of his color, or race, than are prescribed for the punishment of citizens, shall be fined not more than $1,000 or imprisoned not more than one year, or both.

Title 18, U.S. Criminal Code, Section 243

No citizen possessing all other qualifications which are or may be prescribed by law shall be disqualified for service as grand or petit juror in any court of the United States, or of any State on account of race, color, or previous condition of servitude; and whoever, being an officer or other person charged with any duty in the selection or summoning of jurors, excludes or fails to summon any citizen for such cause, shall be fined not more than $5,000.

Title 18, U.S. Criminal Code, Section 594

Whoever intimidates, threatens, coerces, or attempts to intimidate, threaten, or coerce, any other person for the purpose of interfering with the right of such other person to vote or to vote as he may choose, or of causing such other person to vote for, or not to vote for, any candidate for the office of President, Vice President, Presidential elector, Member of the Senate, or Member of the House of Representatives, Delegates or Commissioners from the Territories and Possessions, at any election held solely or in part for the purpose of electing such candidate, shall be fined not more than $1,000 or imprisoned not more than one year, or both.

Title 18, U.S. Criminal Code, Section 3052

The Director, Associate Director, Assistant to the Director, Assistant Directors, inspectors, and agents of the Federal Bureau of Investigation of the Department of Justice may carry firearms, serve warrants and subpoenas issued under the authority of the United States, and make arrests without warrant for any offense against the United States committed in their presence, or for any felony cognizable under the laws of the United States if they have reasonable grounds to believe that the person to be arrested has committed or is committing such felony.

Title 42, U.S. Civil Code, Section 1983

Every person who, under color of any statute, ordinance, regulation, custom, or usage, or any State or Territory subjects, or causes to be subjected, any citizen of the United States or other person within the jurisdiction thereof to the deprivation of any rights, privileges, or immunities secured by the Constitution and law, shall be liable to the party injured in an action at law, suit in equity, or other proper proceeding for redress.

Title 42, U.S. Civil Code, Section 1985 (3)

If two or more persons in any State or Territory conspire . . . for the purpose of depriving, either directly or indirectly, any person or class of persons of the equal protection of the laws, or of equal privileges and immunities under the laws, or for the purpose of preventing or hindering the constituted authorities of any State or Territory from giving or securing to all persons within such State or Territory the equal protection of the law. . . .

. . . if one or more persons engaged therein do, or cause to be done, any act in furtherance of the object of such conspiracy, whereby another is injured in his person or property, or deprived of having and exercising any right or privilege of a citizen of the United States, the party so injured or deprived may have an action for the recovery of damages, occasioned by such injury or deprivation, against any one or more of the conspirators.

Title 42, U.S. Civil Code, Section 1986

Every person who, having knowledge that any of the wrongs conspired to be done, and mentioned in section 1985 of this title, are about to be committed, and having power to prevent or aid in preventing the commission of the same, neglects or refuses so to do, if such wrongful act be committed, shall be liable to the party injured . . . for all damages caused by such a wrongful act. . . .

Index

QUADRANGLE PAPERBACKS

American History

James Truslow Adams. *Provincial Society, 1690-1763*. (QP403)
Frederick Lewis Allen. *The Lords of Creation*. (QP35)
Lewis Atherton. *Main Street on the Middle Border*. (QP36)
Thomas A. Bailey. *Woodrow Wilson and the Lost Peace*. (QP1)
Thomas A. Bailey. *Woodrow Wilson and the Great Betrayal*. (QP2)
Charles A. Beard. *The Idea of National Interest*. (QP27)
Carl L. Becker. *Everyman His Own Historian*. (QP33)
Barton J. Bernstein. *Politics and Policies of the Truman Administration*. (QP72)
Ray A. Billington. *The Protestant Crusade*. (QP12)
Allan G. Bogue. *From Prairie to Corn Belt*. (QP50)
Kenneth E. Boulding. *The Organizational Revolution*. (QP43)
Robert V. Bruce. *1877: Year of Violence*. (QP73)
Roger Burlingame. *Henry Ford*. (QP76)
Gerald M. Capers. *John C. Calhoun, Opportunist*. (QP70)
David M. Chalmers. *Hooded Americanism*. (QP51)
John Chamberlain. *Farewell to Reform*. (QP19)
Arthur C. Cole. *The Irrepressible Conflict, 1850-1865*. (QP407)
Alice Hamilton Cromie. *A Tour Guide to the Civil War*.
Robert D. Cross. *The Emergence of Liberal Catholicism in America*. (QP44)
Richard M. Dalfiume. *American Politics Since 1945*. (NYTimes Book, QP57)
Carl N. Degler. *The New Deal*. (NYTimes Book, QP74)
Chester McArthur Destler. *American Radicalism, 1865-1901*. (QP30)
Robert A. Divine. *American Foreign Policy Since 1945*. (NYTimes Book, QP58)
Robert A. Divine. *Causes and Consequences of World War II*. (QP63)
Robert A. Divine. *The Cuban Missile Crisis*. (QP86)
Robert A. Divine. *The Illusion of Neutrality*. (QP45)
Elisha P. Douglass. *Rebels and Democrats*. (QP26)
Melvyn Dubofsky. *American Labor Since the New Deal*. (NYTimes Book, QP87)
Arthur A. Ekirch, Jr. *Ideologies and Utopias*. (QP89)
Harold U. Faulkner. *The Quest for Social Justice, 1898-1914*. (QP411)
Carl Russell Fish. *The Rise of the Common Man, 1830-1850*. (QP406)
Felix Frankfurter. *The Commerce Clause*. (QP16)
Edwin Scott Gaustad. *The Great Awakening in New England*. (QP46)
Ray Ginger. *Altgeld's America*. (QP21)
Ray Ginger. *Modern American Cities*. (NYTimes Book, QP67)
Ray Ginger. *Six Days or Forever?* (QP68)
Evarts B. Greene. *The Revolutionary Generation, 1763-1790*. (QP404)
Gerald N. Grob. *Workers and Utopia*. (QP61)
Louis Hartz. *Economic Policy and Democratic Thought*. (QP52)
William B. Hesseltine. *Lincoln's Plan of Reconstruction*. (QP41)
Granville Hicks. *The Great Tradition*. (QP62)
Stanley P. Hirshson. *Farewell to the Bloody Shirt*. (QP53)
Dwight W. Hoover. *A Teacher's Guide to American Urban History*. (QP83)
Dwight W. Hoover. *Understanding Negro History*. (QP49)
Frederic C. Howe. *The Confessions of a Reformer*. (QP39)
Harold L. Ickes. *The Autobiography of a Curmudgeon*. (QP69)
William Loren Katz. *Teachers' Guide to American Negro History*. (QP210)
Burton Ira Kaufman. *Washington's Farewell Address*. (QP64)
Edward Chase Kirkland. *Dream and Thought in the Business Community, 1860-1900*. (QP11)
Edward Chase Kirkland. *Industry Comes of Age*. (QP42)
Herbert S. Klein. *Slavery in the Americas*. (QP84)
Adrienne Koch. *The Philosophy of Thomas Jefferson*. (QP17)
Gabriel Kolko. *The Triumph of Conservatism*. (QP40)
Aileen S. Kraditor. *Up from the Pedestal*. (QP77)
John Allen Krout and Dixon Ryan Fox. *The Completion of Independence, 1790-1830*. (QP405)
Walter LaFeber. *John Quincy Adams and American Continental Empire*. (QP23)
Lawrence H. Leder. *The Meaning of the American Revolution*. (NYTimes Book, QP66)
David E. Lilienthal. *TVA: Democracy on the March*. (QP28)